GOD IS CALLING

Leader's Guide

Judith Dunlap and
Mary Cummins Wlodarski

ST. ANTHONY MESSENGER PRESS
Cincinnati, Ohio

Nihil Obstat: Rev. Nicholas Lohkamp, O.F.M.
Rev. Edward J. Gratsch

Imprimi Potest: Rev. John Bok, O.F.M., Provincial

Imprimatur: Most Reverend Carl K. Moeddel, V.G.
Archdiocese of Cincinnati, July 22, 1997

Scripture citations are taken from the *New Revised Standard Version Bible*, copyright ©1989 by the Division of Christian Education of the National Council of Churches of Christ in the U.S.A. and used by permission.

The excerpts from the English translation of *Rite of Christian Initiation of Adults*, copyright ©1974, and the Nicene Creed, excerpted from the English translation of the *Roman Missal*, copyright ©1969 by International Committee for English in the Liturgy, Inc., are used with permission. All rights reserved.

Cover and interior illustrations by Steve Erspamer, S.M.
Cover, book design and line drawings by Sanger & Eby Design

ISBN 0-86716-293-7
Text copyright ©1998, Judith Dunlap and Mary Cummins Wlodarski
Cover and interior illustrations copyright ©1998, Steve Erspamer, S.M.
All rights reserved.

Published by St. Anthony Messenger Press
Printed in the U.S.A.

Contents

PART ONE: USING *GOD IS CALLING*

Introduction   **3**

A Child's Faith   3

A Hands-on Resource   4

Why Family Catechesis?   4

Passing on Faith and Values to Our Children   5

Catechesis for Children Today   6

Story, Personal Witness and Ritual   7

An Overview of the Series   **11**

How to Use the Series   11

Story Objectives, Themes and References
   to the *Catechism of the Catholic Church*   13

Practical Helps   **23**

Communicating the Vision   23

Identifying Parish Needs   23

Tailoring the Program   23

Getting the News Out   24

Getting Help   24

Intergenerational Family Catechesis   **27**

    Adaptions of the Intergenerational Program   28

    Meeting Topics   28

    Adapting *God Is Calling* to the Liturgical Year   31

PART TWO: SUGGESTED LESSON PLANS

Year One: *Yahweh Calls*   **34**

    Session One: 'Yahweh'   35

    Session Two: 'A Chosen People'   38

    Session Three: 'The Promised Land'   40

    Session Four: 'Kings and Queens'   42

    Session Five: 'Prophets and Heroes'   44

    Session Six: 'The Promised Messiah'   46

Year Two: *Jesus Lives*   **51**

    Session One: 'Who Is Jesus?'   52

    Session Two: 'Friends of Jesus'   55

    Session Three: 'The Parables of Jesus'   57

    Session Four: 'The Miracles of Jesus'   59

    Session Five: 'The Last Days of Jesus'   61

    Session Six: 'Jesus Is Alive'   63

Year Three: *Spirit With Us*   **65**

    Session One: 'Pentecost: The Day the Spirit Came'   66

    Session Two: 'Spirit of Belonging'   69

    Session Three: 'Spirit of Prayer'   71

    Session Four: 'Spirit of Forgiveness'   75

    Session Five: 'Spirit of Action'   77

    Session Six: 'The Not-the-End'   79

PART THREE:
INITIATING CHILDREN OF CATECHETICAL AGE

An Overview of the Process   **83**

    Precatechumenate   83

    Catechumenate   83

    Purification and Enlightenment   83

    Mystagogia   83

    Children's Catechumenate and Catch-up Catechesis   84

Adapting the Series for Children's Catechumenate   **85**

    Another Approach to the Catechumenate   87

    The Presentation of the Our Father and the Creed   87

        The Our Father   88

        The Creed   89

    A Penitential Rite With Families   90

    Prayers of Intercession   90

PART FOUR: FAMILY RETREATS

Sharing Stories Retreat   92

Advent Retreat   99

Jesus Retreat   119

Signs, Symbols and Sacraments Retreat   141

Further Resources From St. Anthony Messenger Press   151

Part One

Using *God Is Calling*

The Components of the Series

Storybooks

Yahweh Calls
   (Young Children and Ages 11 to 14)
Jesus Lives
   (Young Children and Ages 11 to 14)
Spirit With Us
   (Young Children and Ages 11 to 14)

Activity Books

Together Time: Yahweh Calls
   (Young Children and Ages 11 to 14)
Together Time: Jesus Lives
   (Young Children and Ages 11 to 14)
Together Time: Spirit With Us
   (Young Children and Ages 11 to 14)

Three Ways to Use the Series

- Intergenerational Family Catechesis
- Children's Catechumenate
- Catch-up Catechesis

Introduction

This *Leader's Guide* offers an overview of the material and programs that are available to you in the series "God Is Calling." It also includes the theological, pedagogical and catechetical underpinning of the series, as well as practical help in introducing and facilitating the program in your parish. There is a separate section for each of the programs in which the series can be used, as well as alternative suggestions for each program.

The series "God Is Calling" is primarily intended to be an intergenerational catechetical series. Its focus is centered on adults and teen faith development as well as that of children. It can be used as a family series in the broadest parochial sense of the word *family*. It can also be used as a resource for children and adolescents who are a part of the catechumenate process. Finally, the series is an excellent resource for families who are just returning to the Church. It is catch-up catechesis at its best. It allows young people to join in the regular parish catechetical program while at home they listen to and reflect on many of the stories that make up the foundation of what they are learning at the parish.

As John Shea says in *Stories of God*,

> To tell a story of God is to create a world, adopt an attitude, suggest a behavior. But stories are first; we are second. We are born into a community of stories and storytellers. In interpreting our traditional stories of God we find out who we are and what we must do. In telling the stories of God we ourselves are told.

There is nothing like a really good story to bring people of all ages together. Chairs circle closer; chins rest on hands as young and old lean forward in anticipation. And when the story is finished the reaction begins. Some have questions; some make comments and explanations as each person looks inside the story and discovers the universal truth the story helped them touch and experience.

The "God Is Calling" series offers thirty really good stories that allow the reader or listener to travel through thousands of years of salvation history. It includes the stories of Adam and Eve, Abraham and Sarah, Esther and Daniel. It retells stories from Jesus' life, about the disciples and saints, early and contemporary. These are all exciting stories of how God has lived and been revealed in the lives of the people. They are stories of faith, right down to the last story in the book, the readers' own story, their part in the ongoing story of the Church.

The catechetical series "God Is Calling" is all about stories and community. It offers families an opportunity to listen to the traditional stories of God that form the foundation of our Christian faith. It is also a simple, enjoyable way for children and adults to listen to each other's stories and explore their own faith. Finally, it gives families of all sizes and descriptions a chance to get together and receive the support and affirmation so needed in today's world.

A Child's Faith

From the moment of birth, children are invited by God into a lifelong relationship. Newborn cries and infant coos are their first response to that invitation. In their first conscious moments, they begin to reach out to the loving God who created them. With their first wondering questions they begin the ongoing process of reflection on their own life experiences: "Why is the sky blue? What makes the grass grow? Where do the stars go during the daytime?" Part of the growth process in every youngster is to ask those faith-centered questions and begin the internal dialogue that will, we hope, continue for a lifetime.

A child's faith life is as vital to personal identity at ages five or six, for example, as at any other time in life. How that life is nurtured and sustained, however, is very much dependent on outside influences. And no influence is greater than that of the child's parent. If there is one thing of which we are absolutely certain, it is this: The family lays the foundation and helps form the infrastructure of a child's faith life.

Families, of course, come in all sizes and in a variety of forms. They can be single-parent, blended or traditional. They may include grandparents, aunts, uncles or foster parents, one or many youngsters. No matter their makeup, all families are important. For better or worse, they are the foundation of every child's moral and faith life.

Families are crucial to the faith development of the next generation, and a faith-filled next generation is crucial to the future of our Church. This is the premise on which the series "God Is Calling" is based.

While we hope this series will be used primarily within a family setting, it can also be used in the more traditional parish catechetical setting as long as young people have willing adult mentors. While this situation is not ideal, it is workable.

A Hands-on Resource

The "God Is Calling" series is a hands-on resource. It can be used with the families of children who are about to be baptized or children whose families are just returning to the Church. It is primarily meant as a tool for families whose children have already been involved in catechesis over the years. Please note that the hyphenated word *hands-on* is plural. The

material is meant to be in the hands of both children and the adults who are important in their lives.

Often parents and adults will do for children what they will not take the time to do for themselves. Sometimes the best adult education happens when parents, guardians, sponsors or mentors are involved in educating youngsters. In the process of helping a young person learn what it means to be a Christian, adults often discover new insights or even rediscover the mystery of their own faith. "God Is Calling" is not just for children. It is family catechesis, a catechetical series for all ages.

Why Family Catechesis?

Look at the faces of the people who make up our parish congregations. Where are the young adults and teens whom we baptized as babies? How many of our parish ministers and volunteers are under the age of thirty? What will the Church be like in another ten or twenty years?

We need to take a serious look at how we are educating, initiating and integrating our children into our Church. What used to work does not seem to be working anymore. We need to find a new approach to catechesis.

Our world and our culture changed dramatically in the last third of the twentieth century. According to national statistics, homicide and suicide rates for young people have tripled in the last two decades. At a time when young people need faith more than anything else, catechetical leaders struggle to discover the key that will help them open up the treasure with which each youngster has already been gifted.

In many parishes, DRE's, catechists and Catholic school teachers spend hours working on lesson plans designed to "teach" children their faith. In today's world, the old adage, "Faith is caught, not taught," carries more weight than ever. The classroom model of religious education can no longer stand on its own. Today parishes and parents have to work hand in hand to help youngsters grow in the faith with which they were blessed at Baptism. Religious education programs that worked in the past are no longer enough to ensure that our children will grow up to be faithful, faith-filled disciples of the Lord. To understand how we got where we are it may be helpful to take a brief look at how catechesis has developed over the last century and a half.

Parents and the faith community have always shared the responsibility of handing on their beliefs and values to the next generation. Parents were usually recognized as the primary people responsible for this essential task. Only recently in the history of our Church did this responsibility seem to shift.

Passing on Faith and Values to Our Children

In the earliest days of our own country's history, immigrant parents taught their children their prayers and their catechism. From time to time the parish priest would come by to test the little ones, asking catechism questions and listening to the answers.

By the mid-nineteenth century, a standardized public education system had developed throughout our country. Children were required by law to attend school. At that time the predominant culture in the United States centered on three basic principles: republicanism, Protestantism and capitalism. The public school system was designed to promote this ideology.

In an era when the differences between Catholics and Protestants received greater emphasis than their common ground, the public schools were basically Protestant. Every day children, no matter what their faith, were required to read the Protestant Bible, pray the Protestant Our Father and recite the Protestant version of the Ten Commandments.

This did not sit well with the American Catholic bishops or with local pastors. They feared that Catholics would lose their identity as well as their faith. As a result, the Catholic Church began to develop its own school system. An 1884 mandate required every parish to have a Catholic school within two years. Religion classes were set up for children who could not attend a parish school. Bible reading and prayer eventually disappeared from the public schools, but the dual system of public and parochial schools remained.

For a great many years the system worked. The Catholic Church grew and flourished. As an unfortunate side effect, the responsibility for a child's religious education subtly began to shift from home to school. Until the second half of the twentieth century, this shift was gradual and seemed harmless. Only in the last few decades did we begin to experience the downside of classroom-based catechesis.

Three events in the 1960's had a significant influence on the American Catholic world: John F. Kennedy's election as president, the Vietnam War and Vatican II. Kennedy's election was a milestone for American Catholics, who had been at the very bottom of the economic, social and political totem pole for the first two centuries of our country's history. Vietnam opened up the global world to the American public. People began seriously to question our political system and the media brought all of this into our living rooms on a daily basis. Finally, Vatican II began to change the very image we had of ourselves as Church. We began to speak about collegiality and "the people of God." Windows opened that could never quite be shut again. And the "people of God," instead of just reciting rote answers, began to question.

In *Will Our Children Have Faith?* John Westerhof reminds us that a number of institutions once helped parents pass on their faith and values to their children: the extended family, the neighborhood, the entertainment industry, and the parochial schools and religious education programs.

In most cases members of extended families lived close to each other. Grandparents, aunts and uncles could support parents in passing on traditions and values. Baptisms and First Communions were celebrated as family milestones.

Children grew up believing in God because everybody believed in God. Some lived in ethnic Catholic neighborhoods where everyone was not only Catholic but also Italian or Irish or Polish. Others lived in neighborhoods with a diversity of faiths, but on weekends everyone went to some church or synagogue. Everyone was something. Being Catholic was a part of a child's self-identity.

The entertainment industry also supported parents in handing on faith and values. The music young people listened to, the movies and television they watched supported basic Judeo-Christian values. Good was rewarded; bad was punished; a good-night kiss or a punch was the extent of the sex and violence young people saw.

Our culture has changed significantly. The existence of God is no longer a given, and churchgoing is not a priority in many households. Jobs move people farther and farther from extended families. Neighbors no longer share responsibility for all the kids on the block. And the entertainment industry, for the most part, no longer supports basic Judeo-Christian values. Many of the books our children read, the music they hear, the television shows and movies they watch suggest a life-style diametrically opposed to those values. A system that seemed to have worked for a century and a half is no longer working.

Of all of the institutions that helped pass on the faith to children, only two are left: parents and the parish religious education program. Those of us who work in catechesis need to take this reality seriously. It is time to rethink how we approach children's religious education in our parishes. Most importantly, it is time to help parents reclaim their primary role in that education.

Yet we must also remember that each family is unique; each family has different needs and varied resources. We often have no way of knowing what demands of time and energy stress a particular family. While it is important to affirm and encourage parents and guardians as they assume responsibility in the faith development of their children, we have to take care not to send already overburdened families on guilt trips. Therefore it is important to make sure parents and guardians understand that they can adapt any of the activities in the series to the needs and schedules of their families.

Catechesis for Children Today

The parish community needs to do more than simply provide classes that teach children about their faith. We also need to help them recognize and identify with that faith. At one time it may have been enough to teach children to be faithful Catholics, but today we need to do more. We need to help children become faith-filled Catholics, to create opportunities for youngsters to experience the faith they were (or are about to be) gifted with in Baptism. Even more importantly, we need to encourage parents and guardians to create an environment at home that does the same.

There is no question that young people need to learn about their religion. An important part of every parish education program will always involve answering questions and providing young people with a vocabulary to express their faith. But catechesis involves more than acquiring theological knowledge. Its primary purpose, according to the *National Catechetical Directory*, is to help one lead a living, conscious and active faith life (see NCD #32). Catechesis involves the head and the heart; it is formational as well as educational.

Catechesis begins early and continues throughout life. This developmental process involves pre-evangelization, evangelization and, finally, the formal catechesis that can happen in a classroom setting. Indeed, if one has not been "formed" in the faith, formal catechesis is impossible and even the best religious education program becomes merely an academic endeavor.

Pre-evangelization creates an atmosphere of trust so that people, both young and old, feel comfortable enough to ask the age-old questions that lie at the heart of being human. Evangelization involves helping people experience the beginnings of faith (NCD #34) by hearing God's invitation to a lifelong relationship. It means helping them to connect their own life stories to the community's stories and Scriptures.

Pre-evangelization and evangelization can happen anywhere—from Grandma's kitchen to neighborhood swing sets. But today's parish needs to create deliberate and intentional opportunities for pre-evangelization and evangelization. Even more importantly, catechetical leaders need to help families understand the vital role they play in evangelizing their children. Indeed, our most important task is often pre-evangelizing and evangelizing the adults themselves.

Formal catechesis (learning about one's faith) can only happen after one has been evangelized, and evangelization can only happen after one has been pre-evangelized. No matter how faithful we are or how well schooled in our faith, we never outgrow the need for all three elements of ongoing catechesis. The process is usually most successful if at every stage and on every level it involves story, personal witness and ritual.

Story, Personal Witness and Ritual

This is the time-honored formula for catechesis. For centuries the faith was handed down as children listened to the stories the elders never tired of telling. For centuries the faith was handed down as elders and children joined together in prayer and ritual. Generation after generation shared their faith in words and actions. And the mystery of God and God's people unfolded in the telling and doing. Our faith survived because believing people told

youngsters the stories, shared their faith and invited them to take part in the rituals.

The blend of story, personal witness and ritual is also the format for the series "God Is Calling." It offers an opportunity for adults and children to share the Church's stories as well as their own. It allows time for them to listen to each other as they discover new facets of their faith. It invites adults and children to pray together and experience the wonder of ritual.

Story. How did you come to believe in God? How did you learn who God was or what it meant to have faith? Why do you still believe today? For most Christians the answer to these questions can be found in a story. The main character of the story may be a devout mother, a lively sister or a compassionate teacher. The plot and the climax may involve a birth, a death, a quiet "ah-ha" moment or a loud "Eureka!" But there is usually a story, a story of how you came to believe and why you believe even today.

One of the most consistent things we hear from anthropologists and sociologists alike about early civilizations is the importance of story. The elders transmitted their wisdom orally. Pictures and written symbols of words followed. Finally, complex alphabets and literary methods developed. Families, cultures, whole nations cherish stories that give meaning and identity and a sense of unity. Reading the history of our country makes us proud of our achievements and aware of our shortcomings. Our stories help us to see ourselves as a people with a certain heritage.

Our Catholic religious tradition also cherishes stories. The most significant stories are in Scripture, both Old Testament (Hebrew Scripture) and New (Christian Scripture). These are the stories of God's own self-revelation. They are the stories of our ancestors in faith, the men and women whose lives and commitments continue to teach us important truths.

There are other stories as well: community stories bound in tradition and lived out in the sacraments and rituals of our Church. The eucharistic Institution Narrative ("On the night before he was betrayed...") centers us in our promise to remember Jesus each time we celebrate his continuing presence with us. The laying on of hands in Anointing or Reconciliation ties us directly to Jesus' healing.

The stories of our culture and our experience affect how we see ourselves and others for good or ill. In our day-to-day lives we feel God's presence most closely—or feel God's apparent absence most poignantly. Our stories of friendship and love, courage and crisis, patience and commitment are the seed of God's Spirit in our lives. When we take the time to examine these personal stories, share them with others and include them in our prayer lives, they too become living testaments.

Which of these, Scripture or tradition, experience or culture, make up the stories of theology, the study of God? All of them! "God Is Calling" offers opportunities for adults and young people alike to hear, tell, expand and learn these stories of faith. The storybooks draw on Scripture and the lives of our Church's heroes, heroines and saints. The discussions in the activity books allow participants to add their own stories. This is an essential part of the catechetical process. If we lose the importance of our own stories, then faith will seem detached and irrelevant. When we integrate our own stories into Scripture and tradition, faith is alive! And when we share those stories with others we become personal witnesses to that faith.

Personal Witness. Sharing one's faith in words or actions is what personal witness is all about. There is an old adage that faith is caught, not taught. While preaching and teaching are an important part of catechesis, we often learn more about God and Church by watching others live out their faith and listening as they share their stories.

Each person's experience of God is unique and deeply personal. We can only picture or imagine God through our own limited perceptions. The same is true when we read Scripture. Each person filters the meaning of the story through his or her own experiences. But God is infinitely greater than one person's perceptions or personal history. When we hear how someone "sees" God, our own image of God is broadened. And this is why it is so important that we talk about our faith. We need to say out loud what we believe and what we wonder about. Each person has a piece of a puzzle, a clue to the mystery. When we talk about our personal experiences of God or our viewpoints of Scripture, we are able to put some pieces together, coming closer to the infinite mystery that is God.

Sometimes words are not enough. Have you ever tried to explain to a three-year-old how to tie a shoe? It is almost impossible to do so without taking the shoelace and making those first loops yourself. Something similar happens when you try to explain to someone what it means to be a Christian. Words will take you just so far. In order really to understand what it means to be a disciple of Christ, you need to see one in action. We can define words like community and service, but it is much easier to understand these concepts by watching and experiencing Christian fellowship and self-giving.

Unfortunately, some people find it difficult to talk about something as deeply personal as their faith. Giving witness through word or action is always a risk. But if we want our children to believe in God and share our faith, it is a risk we must take. How will children know God is real unless they hear the adults around them talking about God? How will children know the importance of prayer unless they see the significant grown-ups in their lives praying?

In many cases parents would like to talk to a child about God or their faith but they find it difficult to get started. The *Together Time* activity books were written with these parents in mind. Each session suggests simple questions for adults and children to reflect on and talk about. The questions offer a comfortable, nonthreatening way to ease into faith talk. Many of the sessions also include optional suggestions for Christian action.

Ritual is a customary procedure, "the way we always do it." Every religion, like every family, has its own rituals. Rituals distinguish one faith from another. How a people celebrate their code and creed can tell you a lot about what they believe and how they live out their faith.

The Catholic Church is a Church of rites and order. Each sacrament has its own matter and form. Our mornings and evenings are marked with special prayers. We have marrying and burying rites, special anointings and blessings for all occasions. Our rituals are one of the hallmarks of our faith. They mark us as Catholic.

Rituals also serve as a way of integrating and enculturating newcomers into the faith. For centuries, young people absorbed faith by accompanying their parents to Church rituals.

Rituals also serve to solidify and enhance family life—the Church family or the domestic family. In *Ritual In Family Living* (no longer in print), James H.S. Bossard and Eleanor S. Ball present four positive influences of family rituals: (1) Rituals are *vitalizing*, they say—life-giving not only to the individual but to the family itself. (2) They are *euphoric*: They make people feel good about themselves and about the family. (3) Rituals are *disciplinary*: They teach us the value of patience and order as we wait and anticipate what comes next. (4) Finally, rituals are *adhesive*. They bring us closer together as a family. Rituals are shared experiences repeated and remembered. Bossard and Ball learned that even when individuals spoke in begrudging terms about the family rituals "their parents made them do," it was still evident that they experienced pride and joy in them.

Some family rituals focus on special holidays such as Christmas or birthdays. More often, rituals are just a part of a family's everyday routine. Families have set ways of sitting at table, reading the Sunday paper or saying prayers before meals. The rituals we practice have a way of identifying and defining who we are as family. For this reason it is important to affirm families as they gather around an Advent wreath or bless a Christmas crèche. It is also a good idea to offer simple suggestions or an occasional booklet or pamphlet on Christian family rituals.

In the "God Is Calling" series, families are encouraged to pray together at the end of each session. The rituals offered are simple and short, but they help develop a sense of the sacred. The special value of rituals centered around the family is that they help us celebrate the holy in the sacredness of our own home.

An Overview of the Series

The "God Is Calling" series offers three sets of storybooks written on two different age levels (under ten and eleven to fourteen). *Yahweh Calls* introduces Hebrew Scripture. *Jesus Lives* presents the gospel story—the life, death and resurrection of Jesus. *Spirit With Us* illustrates the work of the Spirit with stories from the Acts of the Apostles, the Epistles and the lives of saints and modern believers.

The accompanying activity books (*Together Time*) are also written for two different age levels. The Grown-up's Pages remain the same in both versions, but the introductory activity and the response pages are different for each age group, allowing families with children in different age groups to read the same story, develop one theme, work together on the same activity and close with the same ritual. Suggestions for involving preschoolers are also included.

The activity books have two main objectives. The first objective is to help both adults and young people explore the message of each story and learn more about themselves, about God and about the faith. The second is to facilitate faith talk among the youngsters and the adults, to provide a process that allows sharing and listening. Each activity book is designed to accompany a particular storybook. The format allows time for prayer, discussion, a shared activity and a closing ritual.

Four pages are devoted to each story: two for the adults and two for the young person. For the adults there is the "Grown-up's Page" and an adult worksheet that corresponds with the session's activity. Young people have their own two pages. One is an introductory activity—a puzzle or maze or some other fun activity that introduces the story or theme—for the child to work while the adult reads over the materials for the session. The other is a worksheet to help the young person articulate thoughts or experiences regarding the session's theme. Adults and young people share their worksheets as part of each session's activity.

Along with the ten stories presented in each book are six introductory chapters, which have only two corresponding pages in the activity book: a Grown-up's Page and an activity worksheet that is meant to be used by all age groups. These introductory chapters are intended to be used in a large group parish setting. The storybooks and activity books are then sent home for parents and children to continue working on together.

How to Use the Series

For Family Catechesis: Ask families to meet as a group six times a year. Between these intergenerational meetings, they read the storybooks at home and complete the corresponding activities in *Together Time*. The series offers a repeatable three-year cycle.

Some families may prefer to work independently, completing all the activities at home. If this option is offered, a staff person, catechist or facilitator should remain in close contact with the family. If more than one family is using this option, the facilitator should meet occasionally with the adults or with the whole family units, both individually and as a group, to keep families connected to the parish and to offer opportunities to meet other parishioners.

For Children's Catechumenate: Invite children interested in joining our faith, along with their families, to participate in a parish intergenerational family program. The program, supplemented by retreat days, offers an excellent way to invite and welcome newcomers into a larger Church community. If "God Is Calling" is a regular part of your parish catechetical program, simply invite interested children and their families to join the ongoing program. If the series is not a regular offering, invite a number of parish families, depending on the number of new members, to join you in welcoming the newcomers to Church life.

Along with the parish gatherings and take-home sessions, the chapter on the Children's Catechumenate includes a special presentation of the Our Father and the Creed, a family penitential rite and four retreats that augment the process: an opening retreat, a retreat for Advent and two retreats for Lent. The final retreat in Lent, designed for those who are about to be initiated, emphasizes the Sacraments of Initiation by focusing on the symbols of water, oil and bread.

For Catch-up Catechesis: The children of families who are returning to the Church can be included in either of the above options. If your parish chooses not to sponsor a family catechetical program, parents who use the storybooks and activities at home on their own should meet regularly with a member of the catechetical staff.

Story Objectives, Themes and References to the *Catechism of the Catholic Church*

Each storybook contains ten stories, each story with its own particular theme. The theme states in one or two sentences the objective for the story. (Adults will find more information about these themes on the Grown-up's Page in the Activity Books.)

Yahweh Calls

Story	Objectives	Themes	*Catechism* References
'Yahweh'	• To recognize and claim God's call to each of us as individuals. • To understand that God's call is an invitation to be in relationship with God.	God calls each of us, inviting us into an ever-deepening relationship of love.	CCC #1, 54, 121-123, 1604, 1765
'In the Beginning'	• To recognize that God is the Creator. • To accept that each of us has special gifts and talents.	God is our Creator and we are each made special and unique.	CCC #337-349, 355-379, 396-401
'A Chosen People'	• To understand that God's invitation to us, the covenant, requires a response from us to come to fulfillment. • To explore ways we can act as "chosen friends" of God.	God invites us into a special relationship. It is up to us to say "yes."	CCC #62-64, 218, 238, 839, 2085
'Yahweh Calls Abraham and Sarah'	• To discuss how the covenant made by Abraham and Sarah applies to us today. • To recognize that, as chosen people, we are each very important.	We are precious to God.	CCC #59, 72, 705-706, 762, 1222, 1716, 2810

Yahweh Calls

Story	Objectives	Themes	Catechism References
'Yahweh Calls Joseph'	• To explore God's faithfulness through discussing the story of Joseph, his trials and his successes. • To discuss how we see God taking care of us in our difficult times.	God will always take care of us.	CCC #288, 301-302, 306-307, 309-14
'The Promised Land'	• To explore the importance of having a "home," a place where we feel safe and wanted. • To see the "promised land" as our heritage as spiritual descendants of the early Israelites.	We all need a place where we feel we belong.	CCC #218-219, 839
'Yahweh Calls Moses'	• To introduce Moses as a leader chosen by God to use his special talents and to introduce the Ten Commandments as a code for living. • To recognize how God can and does use each of us with our individual gifts to further the Reign of God.	God has given each of us special gifts.	CCC #1916-1964, 2056-2074
'Yahweh Calls Ruth'	• To use the story of Ruth as a model for faithfulness and loyalty. • To recognize the importance of trust in our relationship with God and with others.	We are gift to each other. It is important to honor that gift with faithfulness.	CCC #2201-2220, 2232

Yahweh Calls

Story	Objectives	Themes	Catechism References
'Kings and Queens'	• To explain that the greatness of biblical royalty was bestowed by God on those who loved God, not necessarily on the expected or powerful people of the time. • To see ourselves as sharing in this greatness through our gifts and our faith.	Greatness has to do with who we are and not just what we do.	CCC #1701-1705
'Yahweh Calls David'	• To understand that the usual secular standards of power and strength are more limited than God's expectations. • To explore personal strengths and encourage self-esteem, i.e., loving ourselves because we are loved by God.	God sees all our goodness even if others do not.	CCC #1949, 2012, 2578
'Yahweh Calls Esther'	• To use the story of Esther's deep faith and sincere prayer to encourage hope in God. • To make all aware that God is ready to help us be our best, even when we are afraid.	We need God's help to be the person God calls us to be.	CCC #410-412, 1996-2005
'Prophets and Heroes'	• To discuss the roles of prophets and heroes in our salvation history. • To look for examples of prophets and heroes in today's world.	God needs people to keep the world on the right track.	CCC #1928-1942, 2006-2011
'Yahweh Calls Elijah'	• To explore the role of hope in two stories of Elijah the prophet. • To increase our awareness of the need for hope and patience in our own lives, especially in the face of the world's troubles.	We need to answer God's call and wait with patience and hope.	CCC #61-64, 218, 702, 2581-2589

Yahweh Calls

Story	Objectives	Themes	Catechism References
'Yahweh Calls Daniel'	• To become acquainted with the four common types of prayer: petition, contrition, praise and thanksgiving. • To use Daniel's example of faithfulness to encourage our own "connection" to God through prayer.	We need to stay connected to God. Prayer is our way of staying connected.	CCC #2558-2565, 2568-2589
'The Promised Messiah'	• To review the stories of the people of *Yahweh Calls*. • To define *messiah* as "anointed one" and to discuss how Jesus the Messiah still renews our hope in the coming of the Reign of God.	The world needed someone really special to remind it of God's call to live in peace and harmony.	CCC #711-716, 840

Jesus Lives

Story	Objectives	Themes	Catechism References
'Who Is Jesus?'	• To remember that God loves us and that Jesus came to live out that love. • To introduce the many ways we have of talking about and naming Jesus.	Jesus came to reveal who God is, to share God's love and to help us see our part in the Plan of God.	CCC #430-435, 456-460, 512-524
'Jesus Is Born'	• To recognize that even in Jesus' humble birth he was surrounded by love. • To appreciate and celebrate the gift of Jesus to the world.	Jesus' humble birth shows us that love is what people need most.	CCC #461-463, 470, 478, 525-534

Jesus Lives

Story	Objectives	Themes	Catechism References
'Friends of Jesus'	• To realize that Jesus needed good friends in his life just as we do. • To discover what qualities we find in a good friend and recognize those qualities in Jesus.	Jesus needed friends just as we do. Jesus also wants to be our friend.	CCC #541-545, 552-553, 946-953
'Zacchaeus'	• To see in the story of Zacchaeus that Jesus made a point of befriending the outcast. • To think about who Jesus would befriend today.	Jesus wants us to be friends with everyone.	CCC #374, 2010-2011, 2477-2479
'Mary and Martha'	• To understand the importance of taking time out to be with God. • To spend time in prayer by writing a letter to Jesus.	Jesus wants us to spend time with him.	CCC #27-30, 31-35
'The Parables of Jesus'	• To realize that Jesus liked to teach by telling stories. • To introduce some of the parables that Jesus told.	Jesus told stories to teach us about God's love and how we are to help bring about the Reign of God.	CCC #56, 74-79, 546
'The Son Who Ran Away'	• To realize that we make choices every day to love or hurt others. • To understand that even when we make wrong choices God will still love and forgive us.	God will never stop loving us. God will always forgive us when we ask forgiveness.	CCC #1425-1433, 2838-2845
'The Man Who Stopped to Help'	• To recognize and affirm the differences of people throughout the world. • To recognize and affirm our own goodness and the goodness in others.	We are to love our neighbor as ourselves. Our neighbors include everyone, even those who are called enemies.	CCC #1939-1942, 2839-2845

Jesus Lives

Story	Objectives	Themes	Catechism References
'The Miracles of Jesus'	• To understand that Jesus' miracles were part of his Good News. • To realize that we can be miracle workers if we help carry on Jesus' work.	Jesus' love for people produced some surprising actions and miraculous results.	CCC #547-550, 2616
'Bartimaeus'	• To understand that people have not only material but also emotional and spiritual needs. • To recognize the needs of people both close to us and far away.	Jesus is with us in the darkness to help open our eyes to see the needs of those around us.	CCC #1783-1785, 1878-1979
'The Special Picnic'	• To encourage a thankful heart for gifts received. • To encourage a giving spirit for those in need.	When we share what we have as Jesus teaches, surprising things can happen.	CCC #1786-1789, 1831, 1822-1829
'The Last Days of Jesus'	• To review Jesus' life by remembering favorite stories about Jesus. • To recognize that Jesus had enemies who wanted to stop the Good News.	Jesus' life was an example to us. Jesus lived the Good News all through his life, even to his death.	CCC #426-429, 512-521
'Arriving in Jerusalem'	• To understand that Jesus made a choice to go to Jerusalem and face his death. • To discover that being a follower of Jesus is not always easy.	Sometimes it is not easy to be a follower of Jesus. We must do what is right even when it is difficult.	CCC #557-560, 569-570

Jesus Lives

Story	Objectives	Themes	Catechism References
'How Jesus Died'	• To reflect on Jesus' walk to Calvary. • To respond on Jesus' "way of the cross" through prayer.	Jesus died to show us how to live.	CCC #571-591, 595-618, 624-630
'Jesus Is Alive'	• To recognize that Jesus is still alive with us today. • To affirm how we are "Jesus" for each other.	Even death had no power over Jesus. Jesus is alive with us today.	CCC #638-677, 727-730, 988-1004

Spirit With Us

Story	Objectives	Themes	Catechism References
'The Spirit at Work'	• To introduce the role of the Holy Spirit in the Reign of God. • To recognize that the Holy Spirit is an active and motivating force in our lives.	The Reign of God happens whenever we live with love for God.	CCC #683-689, 737-741, 1210-1212
'Pentecost: The Day the Spirit Came'	• To explain why Pentecost is considered the "birthday" of the Church. • To identify the action of the Holy Spirit in our personal history as well as in our communal history.	The Spirit of God is with us, and great things happen when we are open to the Spirit.	CCC #691-702, 731-732
'Spirit of Belonging'	• To introduce the Sacrament of Baptism as initiation into the Catholic Church. • To discuss how we, as Church, welcome and include each other into our community.	The Sacrament of Baptism makes us members of the Church family, the Catholic community.	CCC #705-716, 733-741, 836-838, 1213-1228

Spirit With Us

Story	Objectives	Themes	Catechism References
'Philip and the Ethiopian'	• To explain the evangelical call of our Baptism (to teach all nations) through the story of Philip's teaching and baptism of the Ethiopian. • To become aware of how our Church community reaches out to others.	We need to risk talking about God so we and others can grow in faith and love.	CCC #888-890, 897-913, 1271-1274
'The Maiden Who Finally Found a Home'	• To examine the support offered when we belong to a faith community, using the life of Blessed Kateri Tekakwitha as example. • To identify ways our Church offers us the support and strength we need by making us know we are always welcome.	Belonging to a faith community gives us support and strength.	CCC #790-791, 813-816, 1265-1270
'Spirit of Prayer'	• To introduce the Sacrament of the Eucharist as the primary source of our continuing relationship with our God. • To use Jesus as our model of the need for consistent personal prayer.	The Sacrament of the Eucharist nourishes our relationship with God. There are many different ways to spend time with God in prayer.	CCC #748-750, 758-771, 1322-1327, 2650-2654
'The Church at Home'	• To present some of the earliest history of our communal prayer, especially the house churches and their celebrations. • To examine communal prayer as it benefits the total faith community and as inclusive of all believers.	We gather with others to pray, and the most special of these times is the Sunday Eucharist.	CCC #772-776, 787-789, 1341-1344, 2655

Spirit With Us

Story	Objectives	Themes	Catechism References
'The Woman Who Laughed With God'	• To discuss personal prayer as necessary for growth in faith. • To recognize the rich diversity of types of prayer by examining the life of Sister Thea Bowman.	When we pray individually, we bring back to God the rich diversity of creation.	CCC #781-795, 830-831, 1201, 2659-2660
'Spirit of Forgiveness'	• To introduce the Sacrament of Reconciliation as the healing celebration of God's forgiveness. • To recognize the need for God's forgiveness by honestly examining personal and social sins (the "circles of hurt").	The Sacrament of Reconciliation is the Church's celebration of God's mercy and forgiveness.	CCC #976-983, 1420-1439, 1446
'The Man Who Made Trouble'	• To discuss our need to admit our failures and confess our sins, using Paul and his conversion as our example. • To encourage prayers of contrition as healing elements in our relationships with others and with God.	Each of us sometimes does wrong and must ask for forgiveness.	CCC #1430-1433, 1440-1445, 1451-1455, 2042
'The Soldier Who Had No Enemies'	• To understand our baptismal call to be healers who forgive others, modeled on the life of Saint Maximilian Kolbe. • To explore how our reliance on the forgiveness of God will help us "let go" of hurts to be truly reconciled to others.	We are called by the Spirit of God to forgive others.	CCC #1010-1014, 1435, 1474-1477

Spirit With Us

Story	Objectives	Themes	Catechism References
'Spirit of Action'	• To introduce the Sacrament of Confirmation as strengthening our ability to love as people of involved, committed action. • To discuss ways we can follow Jesus' gospel mandate, relying upon the promised gifts of the Holy Spirit.	The Sacrament of Confirmation reaffirms our baptismal call to act to establish the Reign of God.	CCC #797-801, 849-856, 1285-1305, 1897-1917
'A Letter of Good News'	• To explore our call to be individually responsive to the needs of others, particularly as written in the Letter of James. • To decide upon activities *each of us* can do to help establish justice and compassion in our world.	There are many ways each of us can work individually toward justice and compassion.	CCC #858-860, 946-953, 1309, 2093-2094
'The Bishop for the Poor'	• To explore some events in the life of Archbishop Oscar Romero to find examples of how we are called to be an active community of justice. • To examine ways the Holy Spirit can use the institution of the Church, *all of us together*, to further the Reign of God.	As a community, as a Church, we are involved in bringing the Reign of God about in our world.	CCC #931, 952-953, 1939-1942, 2012-2016
'The Not-the-End'	• To review how the stories in *Spirit With Us* can provide models and insights for our personal lives and for the life of our Church. • To reflect on how the Holy Spirit continues to be alive in our stories and our actions today.	Individually and in community, we are sacraments because we continue to show the Spirit of God in our actions and in our lives.	CCC #836-865, 871-873, 932-933, 2044-2046

Practical Helps

While family-centered catechesis is increasing, perhaps your parish does not yet offer such a program. This chapter is meant to help you start a parish program. Remember to take it slowly. The first step is to build interest and support for your program. The second step is just as important: Make sure you have plenty of help.

Communicating the Vision

The information offered earlier in this manual supplies you with background, theology and objectives. Compare this material with your parish mission statement. All programs, events, classes or workshops must be rooted in the expressed mission of your parish community (see *CCC* #4-10).

If you do not have a parish mission statement, look for other ways to connect your catechesis with the mission of the Church. Perhaps your local diocesan Office of Religious Education or Formation has a mission statement you can use. Perhaps you can write a mission statement, a vision, for your ministry at the parish. Best of all, get together a group of staff and parishioners to write a parish mission statement.

Whichever direction you choose, be sure you and others see catechesis as a crucial part of the mission of the universal Church. Through education and formation we fulfill Christ's commission to reach out to the entire world and spread the Good News!

Identifying Parish Needs

Once you know how your program fits with the parish mission, spend time identifying parish needs. Assess existing programs and see what gaps exist. A good place to begin is with the people who have expressed to you a need for something different. Talk to your parish council and commissions, and ask them to talk to others. Sit with parish staff members and ask their opinions and insights.

You can make these assessments in formal pen-and-paper sessions, focus groups or informal conversations. However you do it, *do not skip this step*. Asking and listening will help you tailor the components of "God Is Calling" to your community's needs. Wisdom abides in the assembly, so don't hesitate to trust it.

Tailoring the Program

This guide is designed to aid you in tailor-making a program that is just right for your parish. Once you've identified your parish needs you can adapt "God Is Calling" to fit those needs. The various uses of this series were outlined in the Overview of the Series (see page 11).

Think of the storybooks, the activity books and this guide as ingredients in a recipe. Add a little more of what you like, take out what you don't and the finished product will be distinctly yours. The main strength of a component-based series is that it has enough flexibility to help you structure an effective and attractive program for your community.

Then, when you're ready to go, get the news out with enthusiasm!

Getting the News Out

Evangelization often begins with our own contagious excitement about programs. Some parents may resist coming to intergenerational or family programs. Make certain that the program is seen as a way of supporting today's families, and a service to the parish.

Whenever you have the opportunity, at parent meetings, or parish gatherings, share the information in the beginning chapters of this guide book. The information in the Introduction section titled "Why Family Catechesis?" (page 4) is often an eye opener for parents. You might also consider sharing pages 7 to 9 of the Introduction, "Story, Personal Witness and Ritual." Taking time to lay this sort of groundwork may make the difference between hearing parents say, "Do I have to come with my kids?" and "When can we get started?"

In this initial time of gathering interest, remind the adults involved that they are just as likely to be learners as they are to be teachers. No matter what our age, we all enrich each others' lives when we share our stories. As the *Catechism of the Catholic Church* points out, all believers are called to hand on the Good News to following generations by professing and living their faith, by sharing with one another and by celebrating their belief in liturgy and prayer (see *CCC* #3). In intergenerational or family-based catechesis, every participant is both teacher and learner, regardless of age. Everyone has stories and insights to share. Persons experienced in multi-age programs will tell you that some of the greatest faith statements come from very young people!

Getting Help

In effect, everyone who participates in family catechesis is actively involved in helping the program run smoothly. Depending on how you design your particular program, however, you will undoubtedly need specific volunteers.

It is always a good idea to spread out the responsibility for catechetical programs among parishioners. This encourages people to see themselves as spiritual leaders in the community. It increases their sense of ownership in the parish. And, not least, it gets a lot more done with less stress on any one individual. The following are some volunteer roles you may wish to consider.

Coordinators. These volunteers head up specific programs for you by taking responsibility for management. Coordinators may open up buildings, arrange for other volunteers, keep track of supplies and so on. You may need to mentor these volunteers for a while before handing over the role. Certainly these people will need to show greater commitment. But in a year or two they may be able to take over a large part of your responsibilities.

Advisory Board. A group of parents who want family-based catechesis can be great support for the professional catechist. Their views and evaluations will add new dimensions to your own. It is a good idea to include some creative people who can help you think of new approaches to the group gatherings. It is especially helpful if members of this board have children of different ages and a teenager is on it as well. If you have coordinators, make sure they are a part of the board.

This group may meet just quarterly. Their task is both to recommend and to evaluate.

Facilitators. The types of facilitators you will need depends on how your parish chooses to use the "God Is Calling" series. You will need *small-group facilitators* when you break down the large-group gatherings in homes or on parish grounds. These people need to be good listeners. Check your diocesan media office for training materials.

If your large-group gatherings include more than thirty or forty participants and you decide to divide the group, you will need *large-group facilitators* to assist you. These volunteers would be responsible for leading the actual session. They need to be good facilitators as well as good catechists and teachers. Choose carefully. It may be a good idea to include these volunteers on your advisory board.

You will need *home facilitators* if you have more than one or two families working on their own—one for every three to four families. Their job is to call the families together at least once or twice a year. They will also keep in regular touch with families to answer questions, offer suggestions and invite them to family retreats and important parish events.

Retreat Teams. "God Is Calling" includes some retreat days, which can be expanded to overnights, if you wish. You will need people to help set the environment, take leadership roles, take care of the food, get supplies and so on. Ideally, this retreat team would reflect the intergenerational character of the program—that is, all ages would somehow help lead the retreat. Even a very young person can introduce an icebreaker or read a prayer.

Sponsors. If you are using "God Is Calling" for children's catechumenate, consider asking parishioners to serve as sponsors. Admittedly, many young people will ask relatives or friends to serve in this role, but those people are often from out of town or otherwise unable truly to go through the program with a young person.

A parish sponsor, in addition to this family sponsor, can represent the "extended family" of the Church.

We also suggest pairing each family presenting themselves or their children for Baptism with a sponsoring family. This mentoring family will initiate contact with the new family, participate with them in as many intergenerational meetings as possible, answer questions and make introductions during family sessions and other parish gatherings.

Hospitality. Anytime you gather, someone should be concerned with making the environment welcoming. Beverages, snacks, soft music, nametags, a prayer table—all these and more can make even the coldest church hall seem warmer. These folks may also send out reminders for the next large-group gathering.

Cleanup. If you can find a volunteer to coordinate cleanup, everyone (including yourself) will probably get home a lot earlier. With someone else in charge of cleanup, you are free to talk to those people who may need a little encouragement or who have a few questions that need answers. This person should know where trash bags and brooms are kept. It will also help if they gently encourage everyone to help.

This is obviously only a partial list. You can decide what else is needed and go from there.

Choosing and Using Volunteers. Once you have a list of what volunteers your program can use, write job descriptions for each position. These need not be long. For example, a job description for a hospitality volunteer could read: "*Skills/Background*: Comfortable with crowds. Welcoming personality. Sense of humor. *Responsibilities*: Set up snacks each session. Arrange for volunteer bakers when needed. Greet participants each evening."

The job descriptions can help you identify people you may wish to invite to serve and can help you interview volunteers who come forward. This will enable you to match the person's gifts with the right volunteer role.

Clearly defined responsibilities will help you to evaluate the work done and eliminate confusion. Nothing is more frustrating for a volunteer than to feel his or her time was wasted. And little is accomplished if no one is sure whose job it is! A volunteer properly prepared, well equipped and lovingly appreciated is one who will serve gladly in his/her role—and will more likely be willing to recommit.

Finally, assign a term to the volunteers' commitment. People who know they are signing up for only one or even two years are more likely to say yes to your request. They can always sign up for another term—and having the option makes it easier to do so.

This will also give you an opening for periodic evaluations. A face-to-face discussion of the program's effectiveness, the volunteers' comfort with it and how you can be of continuing support is crucial. It will keep your program fresh, your volunteers motivated and keep you in touch with all that is (or is not) happening.

Intergenerational Family Catechesis

"Intergenerational" is not some fancy new approach to catechesis or education. Intergenerationally is how we have always lived! Sometimes we separate into more homogeneous age groupings (school grade levels, retirement centers). But families, parishes, society itself are intergenerational institutions.

This series uses the term *intergenerational* to describe an approach that does not segregate learners by age group. Flexible and open to adaptation, the intergenerational program includes six meetings based on the main divisions of each storybook. (Possible adaptations are described on page 28.) These could be large meetings held at parish centers or smaller gatherings held in individual homes. The families do the stories and activities in each division at home.

After an "icebreaker," an introductory activity meant to relax those in attendance, each of these six meetings models the home sessions for the participants. Each time the leader sets the environment, asks the "Getting Started" questions, covers the reading material, facilitates some activity and discussion of insights. Each meeting also incorporates a closing ritual. (Outlines for these eighteen sessions begin on page 33. For more details on how to encourage use of the storybooks and activity books in the home, please refer to the Overview of the Series, pages 11 to 22.)

You may use one or more of these three intergenerational groupings per session:

1) Family groupings bring young people and adults together to work on an experience or a discussion. Leave the definition of family to the participants themselves; it may or may not mean blood relatives. A family is whoever comes together to your program. An aunt and her niece, a grandfather and his grandchildren, a godmother or sponsor and a teenager—all of these may see themselves as the "family" in your program. In today's world of blended, single-parent and multi-generational families, it is best to be open to all possible configurations.

2) Mixed-generational groupings combine adults and young people of different families into small groups. Many activities form people into these groupings (counting off, same-colored nametags, same month of birth, for example) as long as you are careful to balance the number of adults and young people in each group.

This type of grouping has a few advantages. First, young people (especially teenagers!) often listen more attentively to adults who are not their parents. And adults are often much more patient with children who are not their own, perhaps because they feel less responsibility. And, not the least, the young people are exposed to the affection and faith-sharing of a wider portion of their adult community. Can any young person ever have too many adults care about him or her?

3) Homogeneous age groupings break the group into age levels for an activity or discussion. You will need additional adults to lead the preschool, primary, intermediate and teen groups. To maintain the intergenerational approach, begin together, pray together and gather at the end to share key insights.

Adaptions of the Intergenerational Program

Before you begin. Whatever schedule you choose to follow, begin by gathering the families for the introductory retreat, "Sharing Stories" (see page 92). This retreat, which should be offered for new families each year, introduces the importance of storytelling, as well as small- and large-group sharing. It also teaches families to locate Scripture passages, a skill they will need for working at home.

Parish-Based Meetings. Six times a year, gather any interested families at a center in the parish. The lesson plans that follow allow for ninety-minute sessions. You may expand this time allotment to include some social time. In a large gathering (over thirty participants) enlist other adults as facilitators to help prepare the program. Then break the gathering into two or three groups for the facilitators to lead according to the lesson plans. This works especially well if you have other rooms available for use. Icebreakers, prayers and rituals should include the entire group, however large, to encourage community.

Your own community schedules will affect how you divide these six sessions. We recommend meeting in October, November, January, February, March and April. An Advent retreat day or service activity can be added in December, as well as a closing event of some type in May. (But bear in mind that December and May are often very busy times for families.) It is also possible to combine these six sessions in an intensive program: meeting twice a month in January, February and March.

Home- or Neighborhood-Based Meetings. Equally effective are sessions in individuals' homes, whether monthly or bimonthly, year-long or intensive. The lesson plans can easily be adapted to a gathering of three to five families.

This method also has the advantage of creating a kind of small faith community for families. As director, however, you will need to keep in close communication with the volunteer leaders in each home so that they feel supported in this ministry. The Advent and end-of-year retreats, social times and service projects should remain activities of the whole program, a gathering of all the home communities in order to keep the parish community as a focus for these smaller assemblies.

Supplementing Parish Religious Education Programs (PSR or CCD). The best option is to use the intergenerational program as an *alternative* catechetical program. To require participation in this program in addition to a more traditional religious education program would probably guarantee its failure because people would feel overwhelmed; "tried and true" methods are less challenging. Nevertheless, it is possible to integrate elements of the intergenerational approach into the parish religious education program. Seasonal intergenerational gatherings (autumn, Advent, Lent, Easter) could be built on the four "middle" divisions of each of the three books.

Components of this series can also supplement any program. The Storybooks can be used separately to complement programs on Old Testament, New Testament, Jesus and the Church. The retreats in this guide can also effectively be used independently of other program elements.

Meeting Topics

The following charts indicate the topics for the meetings. The remaining stories and activities in each yearly program are done at home between parish gatherings. See the lesson plans (pages 33-80) for more details.

Topics for Meetings

NOTE: Every year schedule in September the "Sharing Stories Retreat" (see page 92) for everyone interested in joining this program as new participants.

Monthly Meetings

Year One: *Yahweh Calls*

October:	"Yahweh"
November:	"A Chosen People"
December:	Retreat day, service project or social
January:	"The Promised Land"
February:	"Kings and Queens"
March:	"Prophets and Heroes"
April:	"The Promised Messiah"
May:	Retreat day, service project or social

Year Two: *Jesus Lives*

October:	"Who Is Jesus?"
November:	"Friends of Jesus"
December:	Retreat day, service project or social
January:	"The Parables of Jesus"
February:	"The Miracles of Jesus"
March:	"The Last Days of Jesus"
April:	"Jesus Is Alive"
May:	Retreat day, service project or social

Year Three: *Spirit With Us*

October:	"The Spirit at Work"
November:	"Spirit of Belonging"
December:	Retreat day, service project or social
January:	"Spirit of Prayer"
February:	"Spirit of Forgiveness"
March:	"Spirit of Action"
April:	"The Not-the-End"
May:	Retreat day, service project or social

The Intensive Model

Year One: *Yahweh Calls*

December: Retreat day, service project or social

January: "Yahweh" and "A Chosen People"

February: "The Promised Land" and "Kings and Queens"

March: "Prophets and Heroes" and "The Promised Messiah"

April: Retreat day, service project or social

Year Two: *Jesus Lives*

December: Retreat day, service project or social

January: "Who Is Jesus?" and "Friends of Jesus"

February: "The Parables of Jesus" and "The Miracles of Jesus"

March: "The Last Days of Jesus" and "Jesus Is Alive"

April: Retreat day, service project or social

Year Three: *Spirit With Us*

December: Retreat day, service project or social

January: "The Spirit at Work" and "Spirit of Belonging"

February: "Spirit of Prayer" and "Spirit of Forgiveness"

March: "Spirit of Action" and "The Not-the-End"

April: Retreat day, service project or social

Home Sessions

Year One: *Yahweh Calls*

Autumn: "A Chosen People"

Advent: "The Promised Land"

Lent: "Kings and Queens"

Easter: "Prophets and Heroes"

Year Two: *Jesus Lives*

Autumn: "Friends of Jesus"

Advent: "The Parables of Jesus"

Lent: "The Miracles of Jesus"

Easter: "The Last Days of Jesus" and "Jesus Is Alive"

Year Three: *Spirit With Us*

Autumn: "Spirit of Belonging"

Advent: "Spirit of Prayer"

Lent: "Spirit of Forgiveness"

Easter: "Spirit of Action"

Adapting *God Is Calling* to the Liturgical Year

There are many ways to incorporate the liturgical year into this program. Use colors of the season for prayer tablecloths or candles (green for Ordinary Time, violet for Advent and Lent, white for Christmas and Easter, and so on).

Rearrange the stories by theme to parallel liturgical readings more closely. Stories that deal most directly with personal relationship with God could be used during Ordinary Time; stories that relate to forgiveness or conversion during Advent and Lent; stories that emphasize community and social action during the Easter season.

The list below suggests one way to arrange stories and lesson plans from the intergenerational program to fit the liturgical year.

Autumn *(Ordinary Time)*:

"Yahweh" *(Yahweh Calls)*
"A Chosen People" *(Yahweh Calls)*
"Who Is Jesus?" *(Jesus Lives)*
"Spirit With Us" *(Spirit With Us)*
"Spirit of Belonging" *(Spirit With Us)*

Lent:

"The Promised Land" *(Yahweh Calls)*
"Kings and Queens" *(Yahweh Calls)*
"Prophets and Heroes" *(Yahweh Calls)*
"The Miracles of Jesus" *(Jesus Lives)*
"The Last Days of Jesus" *(Jesus Lives)*
"Spirit of Prayer" *(Spirit With Us)*
"Spirit of Forgiveness" *(Spirit With Us)*

Advent:

"A Chosen People" *(Yahweh Calls)*
"Who Is Jesus?" *(Jesus Lives)*
"Friends of Jesus" *(Jesus Lives)*
"Spirit of Belonging" *(Spirit With Us)*
"Spirit of Prayer" *(Spirit With Us)*

Easter Season:

"The Messiah" *(Yahweh Calls)*
"Jesus Is Alive" *(Jesus Lives)*
"Spirit of Action" *(Spirit With Us)*
"The Not-the-End" *(Spirit With Us)*

Winter *(Ordinary Time)*:

"The Promised Land" *(Yahweh Calls)*
"Kings and Queens" *(Yahweh Calls)*
"Friends of Jesus" *(Jesus Lives)*
"The Parables of Jesus" *(Jesus Lives)*
"Spirit of Prayer" *(Spirit With Us)*

Part Two

Suggested Lesson Plans

Year One: *Yahweh Calls*

'Yahweh'

Materials Needed: *Yahweh Calls*, nametags, candle, Bible, banner-size piece of fabric with a large hand drawn in fabric or puffy paint (available at any craft shop) or permanent markers, different colors of fabric or puffy paint, pencils, crayons or markers.

Schedule *(90 minutes):*
• Welcome, Set the Environment
  (10 minutes)
• Opening Activity *(15 minutes)*
• Getting Started *(15 minutes)*
• Read the Story *(10 minutes)*
• Discuss the Story *(10 minutes)*
• Together Time Activity *(20 minutes)*
• Closing Ritual *(10 minutes)*

Objectives: To recognize and claim God's call to each of us as individuals.

   To understand that God's call is an invitation to be in relationship with God.

Theme: God calls each of us, inviting us into an ever-deepening relationship of love.

Background for Program Leaders:

1) Read "Yahweh" in both Storybooks.
2) Read the commentary, Theme and Optional Activities on the Grown-up's Pages for "Yahweh" in the Activity Books.

3) Spend some time deciding how you would describe God (qualities, personality, name, relationship and so on). Do your own drawing of God to help you focus on this activity.

Set the Environment. Since this is the first session of the year, be sure to welcome all the participants and ask them to wear nametags. Ask some of the families to help you set up a prayer table with a candle, a Bible and any other symbol you might want. (An artistic representation of God would be especially appropriate for this gathering.) If possible, have some quiet instrumental music playing in the background.

Opening Activity. In family groups (adults with the children they have accompanied), ask each participant to draw a representation of God. The adults will need to help the younger ones. This drawing can be as realistic or as symbolic as they like. Remind them that this is to help us see how we each view God.

   When they are finished have them share them with the whole group (if not too large) or with a small group. Be sure to repeat their names often. ("It's wonderful to see that Angie has drawn a rainbow.") Everyone should get some applause, since there are no wrong answers.

   As people share their drawings, write down some of the qualities and names of God you hear from the participants. This list will come in handy later in the discussion time.

Getting Started. Have each family discuss: To whom do you talk most on the telephone? What do you usually talk about?

Read the Story. Divide the children into age-level groups: preschool and first grade, ages seven through ten, ages eleven through fourteen. Teenagers and adults should sit with each of the groups to assist them. (Teens often enjoy being the leaders of younger groups.) Have the groups read the material appropriate to the ages of their young people. Younger children will need to be read to; the older children may wish to read the section by themselves.

Discuss the Story. Staying in the age-level groups, discuss the material shared.
1) What are some of the different names that we can call God?
2) Take turns filling in the blanks of the following sentences:

If God were a color, God would be _____ because _____.

If God were a toy, God would be a _____ because _____.

If God were a vehicle, God would be a _____
_____
because _____.

Ask teenagers to fill in the following sentences:

If God were a musician, God would be _____
_____
because _____.

If God were on TV, God would be on _____
_____
because _____.

If God played on any sports team, God would play for _____
because _____.

When each group is finished, call them back together and remind them of the list of qualities and names for God they came up with earlier.

Tell them that this God, Yahweh, is calling to each of us today and reaching out to us.

Together Time Activity. It is important to spend time at the first session each year to establish a covenant with the participants. Recording their answers on a flip chart or blackboard, ask everyone what is needed to make these family gatherings successful (participate with an open mind, attend meetings faithfully, listen to each other and so on). Be sure you also list what you and other catechists or leaders are willing to do (provide supplies, prepare material and so on).

Then prepare a banner that you will use all year to symbolize your community and this covenant. Draw a large hand on the banner with fabric or puffy paint or permanent marker. This hand stands for the hand of Yahweh God. Then have each participant come forward and draw his or her hand on the banner somewhere. Be sure each one's name is in the middle of the hand.

Signing the banner is agreeing to stand by the covenant listed on your chart. If possible, type this covenant and mail a copy to each family as an ongoing reminder.

Closing Ritual. Place the Bible reverently on the table. Tell the participants that all the stories they will be reading are found in this holy book. Lift up the Bible with both hands and offer a prayer of thanks:

> "We thank you, God, for the word you have given us. We ask to be open to the teachings of the stories contained here and to the teachings of the stories of our lives. Be with us through this year as we listen for your call. We ask this in confidence through Jesus and your Holy Spirit. Amen."

End with the Sign of the Cross.

Dismissal. Remind everyone to read "In the Beginning" and to do some of the Optional Activities suggested before your next gathering.

Suggested Banner

'A Chosen People'

Materials Needed: *Yahweh Calls*, nametags, candle, Bible, a plant, paper, pencils and crayons.

Schedule *(90 minutes)*:
- Welcome, Set the Environment
  (10 minutes)
- Opening Activity *(15 minutes)*
- Getting Started *(15 minutes)*
- Read the Story *(10 minutes)*
- Discuss the Story *(10 minutes)*
- Together Time Activity *(20 minutes)*
- Closing Ritual *(10 minutes)*

Objectives: To understand that God's invitation to us, the covenant, requires a response from us to come to fulfillment.

To explore ways we can act as "chosen friends" of God.

Theme: God invites us into a special relationship. It is up to us to say "yes."

Background for Program Leaders:

1) Read "A Chosen People" in both Storybooks.
2) Read the commentary, Theme and Optional Activities on the Grown-up's Pages for "A Chosen People" in the Activity Books.

3) Spend some time remembering a time when you felt close to God. Where are you most likely to feel the presence of God: in church, in nature, with others, alone?

Set the Environment. Again welcome the participants and encourage them to use nametags. Ask some families to help you set up a prayer table with a candle, a Bible and any other symbol you want. (A plant or some other sign of life and creation could tie the first two sessions together.)

Opening Activity. With adults and young people divided evenly into groups, ask the participants to step to one side of the room or the other so that two groups are facing each other. It does not matter if the groups are even or not. This activity is just a fun way to look at ourselves. As you name the two poles of choices below, participants must choose one or the other. Point to either side of the room as you name the two choices and ask people to move back and forth to show which choice they prefer. Don't allow anyone to stand in the middle indecisively; do ask at every second or third choice why people have chosen what they have chosen.

Are you more...
...a tent or a hotel?
...a race car or a bicycle?
...a book or a video?
...a spring morning or a summer night?
...a cat or a dog?

...a beauty or a beast?

...a spotlight or a flashlight?

...a candle or a bonfire?

...a player or a fan?

...a letter or a phone call?

Ask the participants, young or older, to add some choices to this list.

Then say something like,

> "We had fun making our selections today, and we may even have learned some things about each other. Just as we choose things in our lives, so God has chosen us. We will talk today about what it means to be chosen or selected by God."

Getting Started. Have each mixed-generation group discuss: Talk about a time in your life when God felt really close to you. Is there any particular place or time of day when you feel closest to God?

Read the Story. Leaving people in their groups, have an adult in each group read "A Chosen People" from *Yahweh Calls* for younger children and a teenager or preteen read it from the Storybook for older youngsters.

Discuss the Story. In these same groups discuss the material shared.
1) What do you think God's special friends would be like?
2) Do you know anyone who seems to be a special friend of God's?
3) Whom do you think God chooses today? Why do you think that?

Together Time Activity. Tell each group,

> "We know ourselves as chosen by God to be God's friends. The Bible is filled with stories of those chosen by God. We need to look around to see where God is acting in our world today.

> These signs of God remind us that God is with us always!"

Ask each group to find some symbols or signs to bring to the prayer table. Be very clear, especially to older children, that these symbols or signs should represent what they see and where they see God, not necessarily where they have been told to look for God. These can be actual items (from their pockets, from outside, from the room where you meet) or drawings or collages.

Each group should show and explain their symbols to the whole community. Then the items are placed on or around the prayer table. When all are finished, be sure to comment on the variety and richness of the symbols.

Closing Ritual. Ask the adults to stand with their young people in their family grouping. Lead them through the following blessing:

> "Today we stand together as your chosen friends, dear God. Help us to know that you are always with us." *(Invite the adults to make the Sign of the Cross on the foreheads of the young people, and ask the young people to do the same to the adults.)*

> "Teach us how to tell others of your love and your invitation to be with you as friends" *(making the Sign of the Cross on each others' lips).*

> "Make us signs of your love in our world" *(making the Sign of the Cross on each others' hearts).*

> "We know you chose us. Help us always to choose you. Open our minds, our lips and our hearts to your words, so that we can come to know and serve you better. Amen."

Dismissal. Remind everyone to read "Yahweh Calls Abraham and Sarah" and "Yahweh Calls Joseph" and to complete the activity pages for these stories before the next gathering.

'The Promised Land'

Materials Needed: *Yahweh Calls*, nametags, candle, Bible, paper, pencils and crayons.

Schedule *(90 minutes)*:
- Welcome, Set the Environment *(10 minutes)*
- Opening Activity *(15 minutes)*
- Getting Started *(15 minutes)*
- Read the Story *(10 minutes)*
- Discuss the Story *(10 minutes)*
- Together Time Activity *(20 minutes)*
- Closing Ritual *(10 minutes)*

Objectives: To explore the importance of having a "home," a place where we feel safe and wanted.

To see the "promised land" as our heritage as spiritual descendants of the early Israelites.

Theme: Everyone needs a place to belong.

Background for Program Leaders:

1) Read "The Promised Land" in both Storybooks.
2) Read the commentary, Theme and Optional Activities on the Grown-up's Pages for "The Promised Land" in the Activity Books.
3) Ask yourself how important "comfort" or "home" is to you. When is the last time you felt truly safe and protected?

Set the Environment. Welcome the participants and encourage them to use nametags. Ask some of the families to help you set up a prayer table with a candle, a Bible and a map, atlas or globe to symbolize the nature of this session and the two following stories. "The Promised Land" is about the travels of the Hebrews and God's promise to give them a home.

Opening Activity. Have every participant find a partner. The very young (under six) or shy may, of course, stay with their adults. But all others should find a partner of an opposite age group. If your gathering is unevenly divided, they may form some groups of no more than three.

Then have each participant close his or her eyes and be led about the room by the partner. Encourage people to cover their eyes with their hands, but do not blindfold anyone! Very young children may find that too frightening, and asking them to remember what made them peek while being led is part of the discussion. If weather permits, this exercise could be done outside.

After each partner spends five minutes being led and five minutes as a leader, gather the group together. Ask these three questions:
1) Was it harder to be led or to lead? Why?
2) Did you peek? Why?
3) Did you have a good leader? What made him or her a good leader?

Tell them,

"The chosen of God were led by God many times into situations and lands that were unknown to them. But God always promised that they would have a home. They had a home in God but they also needed a home here on earth. God had to lead them to this Promised Land."

Getting Started. Have these mixed-generation partners sit down to discuss these questions with each other: What do you think is the most comfortable space in your home? Why? Where do you go when you want to be alone and feel safe? Why?

Read the Story. Have the adult or teenager in each pair read "A Chosen People" from the age-appropriate Storybook.

Discuss the Story. Have each set of partners find two more sets of partners (making groups of six to nine people) to discuss the material shared.
1) What do you think the Promised Land will look like?
2) How will settling in the Promised Land change the lives of the Chosen People?
3) If you could live anywhere, where would your Promised Land be?

Together Time Activity. Tell each of these small mixed-generation groups:

"What would make a truly comfortable room in your opinion? Think not only about what would be in the room, but how the room would be decorated, lit, colored and so on. In your small group decide what a comfortable and safe room would look like to you all. Then, with one of you acting as interior decorator, use each other to make this room. Participants may act as pieces

of furniture, lamps, tables, accessories, other people—whatever!"

After each group shows its dramatic presentation, ask the participants how they can feel so comfortable in God. (For example, someone who is a large, cozy chair might say that the comfort comes from being softly supported.) Draw parallels between their insights of "home" and images of God.

Closing Ritual. As the families learned last time, signing our heads, lips and hearts are symbols of our willingness to be open to God's word. Begin this ritual by asking all participants to sign their own foreheads, lips and hearts as you pray:

"We know you chose us. Help us always to choose you. Open our minds, our lips and our hearts to your words, so that we can come to know and serve you better."

Read Genesis 17:3-8. Ask the young people to say whatever prayers are in their hearts, aloud or in the silence of their hearts. Close with the Sign of the Cross.

Dismissal. Remind everyone to read "Yahweh Calls Moses" and "Yahweh Calls Ruth" and to complete the activity pages for these stories before your next gathering.

'Kings and Queens'

Materials Needed: *Yahweh Calls*, nametags, candle, Bible, poster boards, markers, magazines, newspapers, glue, paper, pencils and crayons.

Schedule *(90 minutes)*:
• Welcome, Set the Environment *(10 minutes)*
• Opening Activity *(15 minutes)*
• Getting Started *(15 minutes)*
• Read the Story *(10 minutes)*
• Discuss the Story *(10 minutes)*
• Together Time Activity *(20 minutes)*
• Closing Ritual *(10 minutes)*

Objectives: To explain that the greatness of biblical royalty was bestowed by God on those who loved God, not necessarily on the expected or powerful people of the time.

To see ourselves as sharing in this greatness through our gifts and our faith.

Theme: Greatness has to do with who we are, not just what we do.

Background for Program Leaders:

1) Read "Kings and Queens" in both Storybooks.
2) Read the commentary, Theme and Optional Activities on the Grown-up's Pages for "Kings and Queens" in the Activity Books.

3) What comes to your mind when you think of the word royalty? What positive or negative reactions or images do you have?

Set the Environment. Welcome the participants and encourage them to use nametags. Since people should be more familiar with each other by now, you may want to do something different with the nametags. For example, for this session prepared nametags marked "King Dan," "Queen Jane," "Princess Katie," "Prince Philip" could be made for the participants. A good addition to the prayer table could be any sign of royalty: a crown, a coat of arms, some tribal cloth. This symbolizes the nature of this session and the two stories following it.

Opening Activity. Have the participants sit in a circle, with one chair less than the number of people. (Groups larger than twenty should be divided into separate circles.) A volunteer should stand in the middle. This King or Queen gets to make a royal decree, such as, "I order all people wearing blue to go into exile." Everyone wearing blue then has to move to a new seat in the circle. You can't return to your own seat immediately, or to the ones directly to your right or left. The person left standing is the new King or Queen and gets to make the next decree. Decrees can refer to articles of clothing, physical features, hobbies, interests or activities. Avoid embarrassing decrees such as "all smokers."

Take a few minutes at the end of the game to discuss what, if any, new thing your group may have learned about each other.

Getting Started. Have the family groups begin with these questions: Who is someone you think is really great? Why?

Read the Story. Read aloud to the entire group "Kings and Queens" from *Yahweh Calls* for older children. Encourage families with younger children to read the same section for that age when they start to work on the Together Time Activity.

Discuss the Story. Keeping your large group together, ask people to share some of the names of great people they discussed in their families. List these names on half of a flip chart page or large poster. On the other half write why these people are considered great. Explain in your own words:

> "This is a list of what we think makes great people. These qualities and actions make these people kings and queens to us—not in title, but in our respect."

1) What do you think God would expect from a heavenly royal family?
2) What do each of us have inside ourselves that makes us royal, too?

Together Time Activity. Tell each family group that they will be making a coat of arms or crest for themselves. These coats of arms were ways to identify families without words, and they incorporated such things as the family occupation, wealth, land of origin and so on.

Each family should begin by listing some of their hobbies, interests, qualities, jobs or whatever. Then they can look through magazines or newspapers for pictures that capture these and glue them onto the crest, or they can draw symbols or items on the poster board. Each member of the family group should be represented in some fashion on the crest.

The more symbols family members have in common, the better. After all, this is meant to show who "we" are, not just who "I" am.

Take a few minutes to allow families to share their crests with the group.

Closing Ritual. Place the family crests around the prayer table. Remind the participants that while we are not titled royalty, God loves each one of us and expects us to act with respect for all. We are not people caught in the trap of judging what we see on the outside. We know that the greatness we seek is in our hearts.

Make the Sign of the Cross. Then have all hold their hands over their hearts and repeat after you:

> "You know what is in my heart, dear God. Let your name be written there. Make me as strong as the Kings and Queens of your Bible. Amen."

End with the Sign of the Cross.

Dismissal. Remind everyone to read "Yahweh Calls David" and "Yahweh Calls Esther" and to complete the activity pages for these stories before your next gathering.

'Prophets and Heroes'

Materials Needed: *Yahweh Calls*, nametags, candle, Bible, magazines, newspapers, glue, poster boards, flip chart or blackboard, paper, pencils and crayons.

Schedule (*90 minutes*):
- Welcome, Set the Environment
  (*5 minutes*)
- Opening Activity (*20 minutes*)
- Getting Started (*10 minutes*)
- Read the Story (*5 minutes*)
- Discuss the Story (*10 minutes*)
- Together Time Activity (*25 minutes*)
- Closing Ritual (*15 minutes*)

Objectives: To discuss the roles of prophets and heroes in our salvation history.

   To look for examples of prophets and heroes in today's world.

Theme: God needs people to keep the world on the right track.

Background for Program Leaders:

1) Read "Prophets and Heroes" in both Storybooks.
2) Read the commentary, Theme and Optional Activities on the Grown-up's Pages in the Activity Books.)

3) Have you ever wanted to give up? What kept you going? Are there people in your life or in the public view who seem to be genuine prophets or heroes to you?

Set the Environment. Welcome the participants and encourage them to use nametags. Ask some of the families to help you set up a prayer table with a candle, a Bible and perhaps some type of trophy (real or play) to symbolize achievement. "Prophets and Heroes" is about biblical people who accomplished great things.

Opening Activity. Place the name of someone famous, real or fictional, on the back of each participant without letting the person see the name. Be sure to mix your list (famous historical figures, sports figures, media stars, Church figures, people from the Bible), but be sure also to pick *positive* role models. Remember that your very young participants should get names they will be able to identify (Barney or Big Bird as opposed to Pope John XXIII, for example).

   Then each participant asks the others "yes or no" questions ("Am I a woman?" "Am I presently alive?") until they find out who they are. Preschool children may walk with and help an older partner.

   When everyone is finished, ask: Was it easy or difficult for you to identify your person? Is this person someone you admire? Why or why not?

Getting Started. Break into mixed-generation groups to discuss these questions: Have you ever had to speak out about a wrong done in your school or community? Was there ever a time when you were silent and later felt you should have spoken? What happened?

Read the Story. Have each group read "Prophets and Heroes" from whichever Storybook is appropriate.

Discuss the Story. Have one person in each group record the answers to these two questions on a sheet of paper divided in half, one half entitled "Prophets" and the other "Heroes."
   1) What makes someone a hero?
   2) What makes someone a prophet?

Together Time Activity. Ask each group to report their lists to you as you record them on a flip chart or blackboard. Ask them to look over these qualities. Say in your own words:

> "There are still prophets and heroes in our midst today. Using the newspapers and magazines here, look for stories or pictures of people who have the qualities on these lists. Then glue them together in a collage on your group's poster board."

Allow time for the mixed-generation groups to make their creations. Ask them to pick someone who can say a little about what the poster means and to bring the posters with them to the Closing Ritual.

Closing Ritual. Read Isaiah 6:8 aloud. Ask each group to explain what their collage says about prophets and heroes. Then, after each poster is explained, lead the response by saying,

> "I hear the voice of the LORD asking 'Whom shall I send? Who will go for me?'" The gathering responds, "Here I am, God, send me!"

Close with the Sign of the Cross.

Dismissal. Remind everyone to read "Yahweh Calls Elijah" and "Yahweh Calls Daniel" and to complete the activity pages for these stories before your next gathering.

'The Promised Messiah'

Materials Needed: *Yahweh Calls*, nametags, candle, Bible, prayer table symbols from past meetings, copies of "Autograph Hunt" (see page 49), paper, pencils and crayons.

Schedule *(90 minutes)*:
• Welcome, Set the Environment *(10 minutes)*
• Opening Activity *(15 minutes)*
• Getting Started *(15 minutes)*
• Read the Story *(10 minutes)*
• Discuss the Story *(10 minutes)*
• Together Time Activity *(20 minutes)*
• Closing Ritual *(10 minutes)*

Objectives: To review the stories of the people of *Yahweh Calls*.

To define *messiah* as "anointed one" and to discuss how Jesus the Messiah still renews our hope in the coming of the Reign of God.

Theme: The world needed someone really special to remind it of God's call to live in peace and harmony.

Background for Program Leaders:

1) Read "The Promised Messiah" in both Storybooks.
2) Read the commentary, Theme and Optional Activities on the Grown-up's Pages for "The Promised Messiah" in the Activity Books.

3) Do you think the world is good and hopeful or in trouble and beyond hope? Where do you think the idea of Messiah fits in your worldview?

Set the Environment. This is the last session of the year, so you may want to plan some special food or activity. It is always appropriate to celebrate the community you have built together! Ask some of the families to help you set up a prayer table with a candle, a Bible and, if possible, all of the extra symbols you have used this year (map, globe, trophy, plant and so on) to show how much the participants have discussed.

Opening Activity. Since this session is about hope and the future, ask all to spend a few moments thinking about what they plan or hope to do this summer. Then give each person old enough to write (younger folks can team up with older ones) a copy of the "Autograph Hunt" sheet at the end of this lesson. See how quickly they can fill in their sheets.

Getting Started. Break into family groups to discuss these questions:

Did you ever have someone show up at just the right moment to cheer you or support you? How did that feel?

Read the Story. Have each family read "The Promised Messiah" aloud to younger children or quietly to themselves, whichever is appropriate.

Discuss the Story. Ask each family to discuss:
1) Where do you "find" God? Alone? With others? In nature?
2) Are you like any of the people in *Yahweh Calls*? Who?

Together Time Activity. In your own words say,

"The world is not a perfect place. We still have many problems. We still need the Messiah to work with us and through us to bring about the Reign of God. So, let's advertise."

Break the groups into mixed generations for this activity. (Count off or combine families.) Give the following directions:

"First, list what qualities, skills, personal traits you would want in a Messiah. Then list what you could offer the Messiah as support. After the lists are finished, design an ad for a magazine, a billboard, a radio commercial or a TV commercial. Remember to include art work or music or jingles. You don't want a boring Messiah!"

When each group is finished, share the "ads."

Closing Ritual. Gather the group together and lead them in this prayer:

"Compassionate God, you know our world is still suffering and still has problems. We ask you to save us and make us your people." (*Invite the gathering to name aloud any people or issues they want God to save.*)

"Savior God, we know you are with us and have defeated evil. We ask you to remind us to be a grateful people." (*Invite the gathering to name aloud any things or people for whom they are grateful.*)

"Sanctifying God, you know us and we know you. Heal us and bring us to you. Amen."

Dismissal. Remind everyone to complete the activity pages for "The Promised Messiah" and to try the optional activities. Celebrate the year together!

Autograph Hunt

Get the signatures of others beside the activities. No signature can be repeated more than twice.

_____ plans to spend the summer at a pool.

_____ will be playing on a baseball team.

_____ will catch up on computer or video games.

_____ will sit outside with a good book.

_____ will be taking some kind of classes.

_____ plans to travel in our state.

_____ plans to travel out of our state.

_____ plans to travel out of the country.

_____ will work at a summer job.

_____ will work on a garden.

_____ wants to visit other family members.

_____ plans to do some type of volunteer work.

Year Two: *Jesus Lives*

'Who Is Jesus?'

Materials Needed: *Jesus Lives*, nametags, candle, Bible, banner-sized piece of fabric with "JESUS LIVES" drawn in the middle of the banner in fabric paint, puffy paint or permanent marker (see page 54), hearts drawn around the border with spaces between, crosses cut out of cotton or muslin, different colors of fabric or puffy paint, paper, pencils and crayons.

Schedule *(90 minutes)*:
• Welcome, Set the Environment
  (10 minutes)
• Opening Activity *(15 minutes)*
• Getting Started *(15 minutes)*
• Read the Story *(10 minutes)*
• Discuss the Story *(10 minutes)*
• Together Time Activity *(20 minutes)*
• Closing Ritual *(10 minutes)*

Objectives: To remember that God loves us and that Jesus came to live out that love.

   To introduce the many ways we have of talking about and naming Jesus.

Theme: Jesus came to show God's love and to help us see our part in the plan of God.

Background for Program Leaders:

1) Read "Who Is Jesus?" in both Storybooks.
2) Read the commentary, Theme and Optional Activities on the Grown-up's Pages in the Activity Books.
3) What have you been taught about Jesus? What is your experience of Jesus? Is there any name or title for Jesus that is especially important for you? Why?

Set the Environment. Since this is the first session of the year, be sure to welcome all the participants and ask them to wear nametags. Ask some of the families to help you set up a prayer table with a candle, a Bible and any other symbol you want. (An artistic representation of Jesus would be especially appropriate for this gathering.) If possible, have some quiet instrumental or classical music playing in the background.

Opening Activity. Staying in family groups (adults with the children they have accompanied), ask each group to list words they think of when they think about Jesus. If anyone has a favorite story about Jesus, share that too. Then invite each family to stand up, introduce themselves and finish this sentence: "What we like about Jesus is...." Everyone should get some applause, since there are no wrong answers.

   As people introduce themselves and share their insights about Jesus, write down some of the qualities and names of Jesus you hear from the participants. This list will come in handy later in the discussion time.

Getting Started. Have each family discuss this question: What do you think it would have been like to live next door to Jesus?

Read the Story. Divide the children into age-level groups (preschool and first grade, ages seven through ten, ages eleven through fourteen). Teenagers and adults should sit with each of the groups to assist them. (Teens often enjoy leading younger groups.) Each group should read the age-appropriate material. Younger children will need to be read to; older children may wish to read to themselves.

Discuss the Story. Staying in the age-level groups, discuss the material shared.
1) What are some of the names or titles that people sometimes use for Jesus?
2) What do you think Jesus looked like? (Smaller children may wish to draw a picture of themselves with Jesus.)

Together Time Activity. It is important to spend time at the first session each year to establish a covenant with the participants. Recording their answers on a flip chart or blackboard, ask everyone what is needed to make these family gatherings successful (participate with an open mind, attend meetings faithfully, listen to each other and so on). Be sure you also list what you and other catechists are willing to do (provide supplies and prepare material, for example). Then prepare a banner that you will use all year to symbolize your community and this covenant.

Bring out the banner on which you have already written "JESUS LIVES." Give each family a fabric cross. Ask the groups to write the family last name(s) on the center of the cross with paint or markers, then dip each family member's thumb in the paint and press a thumbprint on the cross. Placing this family cross on the banner (they can be pinned on now and glued later) is a sign of agreement to the covenant.

Closing Ritual. Place the Bible reverently on the table. Tell the participants that all the stories they will be reading are found in this holy book. Lift up the Bible with both hands and offer a prayer of thanks similar to this:

"We thank you, God, for the word you have given us. We ask to be open to the teachings of the stories contained here and to the teachings of the stories of our lives. Be with us through this year as we listen for your call. We ask this in confidence through Jesus and your Holy Spirit. Amen."

End with the Sign of the Cross.

Dismissal. Remind everyone to read "Who Is Jesus?" and "Jesus Is Born" and to complete the activity pages for these stories before the next gathering.

'Friends of Jesus'

Materials Needed: *Jesus Lives*, nametags, candle, Bible, Hula-Hoops, slips of paper, flip chart or blackboard, paper, pencils and crayons.

Schedule *(90 minutes)*:
- Welcome, Set the Environment *(10 minutes)*
- Opening Activity *(15 minutes)*
- Getting Started *(15 minutes)*
- Read the Story *(10 minutes)*
- Discuss the Story *(10 minutes)*
- Together Time Activity *(20 minutes)*
- Closing Ritual *(10 minutes)*

Objectives: To realize that Jesus needed good friends in his life just as we do.

   To discover what qualities we find in a good friend and recognize those qualities in Jesus.

Theme: Jesus needed friends, just as we do. Jesus also wants to be our friend.

Background for Program Leaders:

1) Read "Friends of Jesus" in both Storybooks.
2) Read the commentary, Theme and Optional Activities on the Grown-up's Pages in the Activity Books.
3) Do you describe Jesus as your friend? Why or why not? Do you see yourself as a friend to Jesus? Why or why not?

Set the Environment. Welcome all the participants and ask them to wear nametags. Ask some families to help you set up a prayer table with a candle, a Bible and a picture or pictures of some of your friends.

Opening Activity. Divide into two teams of equal numbers. Have each team form straight lines and hold hands. Give a person at the end of each line a Hula-Hoop. Explain that the goal is to pass the Hula-Hoop all the way down the line and then back again to the original spot without letting go of anyone's hand. This means each person has to somehow step into and through the Hula-Hoop so it can pass to the next person in line. Whichever team finishes first wins.

   After the game, discuss briefly what helped the process of passing the hoop and what hindered. (Expect to hear words like *communication, cooperation, patience* and *teamwork*.) Point out that supporting each other is the best way to get things done—and that is what friends do for each other all the time. Jesus was such a friend; he had friends who did that for him, too.

Getting Started. Have each family discuss these questions: Who is the best friend you ever had? Who is your best friend right now? Why? How did you meet? What do you do together?

Read the Story. Have the families read the material appropriate to the ages of their young people.

Discuss the Story. Staying in the family groups, discuss the material shared.

1) What do you think Jesus and his friends did when they were your age? (Adults: Remember that Jesus died young.)

2) What do you think it was about Jesus that made people want to be his friend?

3) Can you name any of Jesus' friends?

Together Time Activity. Break into age-level groups (preschool, six to eight, nine to ten, eleven to thirteen, fourteen and up, adult) with an adult leader sitting in with each group. Each group should come up with a list of ten qualities expected in a friend. (Younger children can draw pictures of times they were with their friends.) Reconvene the large group and share the lists (start with the youngest), recording the answers on a flip chart or blackboard. Ask all to pick a quality that best fits their friendship with Jesus. Have them write this word (or have someone write the word for them) on a slip of paper to bring to the Closing Ritual.

Closing Ritual. Open with this prayer or a similar one:

"Jesus, sometimes we forget that, although you are God, you were also human just like us. You laughed and cried, worried and rejoiced just as we do. You were a friend to those around you; you had friends who cared about you. Help us to be your friends and always to know your friendship for us. Amen."

Then invite all participants to give their friendship word (on the slip of paper) away. When everyone has a new word, have them open up the slips of paper. Encourage them to pray for this quality and to live this quality in the weeks to come. End with the Our Father.

Dismissal. Remind everyone to read "Zacchaeus" and "Martha and Mary" and to complete the activity pages for these stories before the next gathering.

'The Parables of Jesus'

Materials Needed: *Jesus Lives*, nametags, candle, some children's storybooks, large ball of yarn, tape recorders, blank cassette tapes, Bibles or children's Bibles, paper, pencils and crayons.

Schedule *(90 minutes):*
• Welcome, Set the Environment
  (10 minutes)
• Opening Activity *(20 minutes)*
• Read the Story *(10 minutes)*
• Discuss the Story *(5 minutes)*
• Together Time Activity *(30 minutes)*
• Closing Ritual *(15 minutes)*

Objectives: To realize that Jesus liked to teach by telling stories.

  To introduce some of the parables that Jesus told.

Theme: Jesus told stories to teach us about God's love and about how we are to help bring about the Reign of God.

Background for Program Leaders:

1) Read "The Parables of Jesus" in both Storybooks.
2) Read the commentary, Theme and Optional Activities for "The Parables of Jesus" on the Grown-up's Pages in the Activity Books.

3) Is there a story from your life that is especially important to you? Why? What parables of Jesus are your personal favorites? Why?

Set the Environment. Welcome all the participants and ask them to wear nametags. Ask some of the families to help you set up a prayer table with a candle, a Bible and some children's storybooks.

Opening Activity. Ask everyone to stand in a circle. Give one person a ball of yarn large enough to be passed among the group without running out. This person finishes this sentence: "My favorite book/movie/story is _____ because _____." (Model this by starting yourself with an answer that is short, not detailed.) Any other people in the circle who also like this book/movie/story raise their hands. The person holding the ball of yarn holds onto the end of the yarn and throws the ball to someone with a hand in the air. This person catches the ball and repeats the procedure. If no one is holding up a hand, then the person throwing the yarn ball can call a name of anyone who has not yet received the ball and toss it there.

  You should end up with a web-like configuration, each person holding onto the yarn. The ball should finally return to the first person who threw it. Have members pull on their end of the yarn and notice what happens to the whole web. Then place the web carefully on the ground and leave it there for the Closing Ritual.

Stories weave us together just like this web. Stories we have in common, as well as stories that are just ours alone, teach us about each other, about ourselves and even about God.

Getting Started. In this session, the questions were combined with the Opening Activity.

Read the Story. Have each family read the material appropriate to the ages of the young people.

Discuss the Story. Staying in the family groups, discuss the material shared.
1) What do you think it takes to be a good storyteller?
2) What are some things that make a story interesting?
3) Do you know or remember any stories that Jesus told people?

Together Time Activity. Break into mixed-generation groups. Give each group a Bible or a children's Bible, a tape recorder and a blank cassette tape.

Explain that they are to come up with a radio program, a play based on one of the parables of Jesus. Suggest one of the two parables they will be encountering in the coming weeks, the Prodigal Son (Luke 15:11-32) or the Good Samaritan (Luke 10:23-36). But if someone in the group has a different idea, any parable of Jesus will work! The Gospels of Matthew and Luke are good sources for parables.)

Encourage them to include commercial breaks, sound effects and so on. They may do the parable just as written in Scripture or they can create a modern version, but they must keep Jesus' original teaching or purpose.

Give them time to discuss the parable, write their scripts and tape their shows before you come back together and listen to each other's programs.

Closing Ritual. Return to the web on the ground and stand around it again. Open with this prayer or a similar one:

> "Jesus, your stories touch our lives even today. Thank you for all you have given us. Help us to understand your stories so that we can share the Good News. Amen."

Join hands and pray together the Our Father.

Dismissal. The activity pages for "The Parables of Jesus" offer a fun activity for families to complete at home, so encourage them to give it a try. Remind everyone to read "The Son Who Ran Away" and "The Man Who Stopped to Help" and to complete the activity pages for these stories before the next gathering.

Ask all the participants to look for good news in newspaper or magazine articles or TV stories for the next session, especially stories about people making a positive difference in others' lives. (A reminder closer to the meeting date will help.)

'The Miracles of Jesus'

Materials Needed: *Jesus Lives*, nametags, candle, enough vigil candles for each family or participant, Bible, paper, pencils and crayons.

Schedule *(90 minutes)*:
- Welcome, Set the Environment *(10 minutes)*
- Opening Activity *(15 minutes)*
- Getting Started *(15 minutes)*
- Read the Story *(10 minutes)*
- Discuss the Story *(10 minutes)*
- Together Time Activity *(20 minutes)*
- Closing Ritual *(10 minutes)*

Objectives: To understand that Jesus' miracles were part of his Good News.

To realize that we can be miracle workers if we help carry on Jesus' work.

Theme: Jesus' love for people produced some surprising actions and miraculous results.

Background for Program Leaders:

1) Read "The Miracles of Jesus" in both Storybooks.
2) Read the commentary, Theme and Optional Activities for "The Miracles of Jesus" on the Grown-up's pages in the Activity Books.
3) Do you believe in miracles? Before you lead this discussion, you may want to spend some time thinking about how you define miracles and whether you believe they still happen today.
4) Before this session, remind the participants to bring stories, articles or clippings about "good news" events. You may want to have some extras set aside for those who forget.

Set the Environment. Welcome all the participants and ask them to wear nametags. Ask some of the families to help you set up a prayer table with a candle, a Bible and a newspaper or news magazine.

Opening Activity. Give each family a few minutes to read or tell their "good news." Tell them to keep the articles to use later when they do the activity for the story "Bartimaeus."

Getting Started. Ask each family to discuss: Do you recall any big or little "miracles" in your own life—times when it felt like God was giving you some extra help? Have you ever heard someone talk about a miracle in their lives?

Read the Story. Have the families read the material appropriate to the ages of their young people.

Discuss the Story. Staying in the family groups, discuss the material shared.

1) Of the miracles mentioned, which do you think you would have liked to have seen for yourself? Why?
2) If you could ask Jesus for a miracle, what would you ask for?
3) Do you think Jesus ever got tired of being a miracle worker?

Together Time Activity. Break into age-level groups (preschool, six to eight, nine to ten, eleven to thirteen, teens, adults) with adult leaders sitting in with each group. The purpose of this activity is to encourage hope within our community by showing even our youngest members that they can make a difference.

Jesus' miracles had to do with healing and with meeting people's needs. While the preschool children work on drawing ways we can take care of each other, have all the other age groups list problems they see in today's world, in their schools, in their families, among their friends or in the Church community. Then each group should pick one of these problems and decide what they can do about it.

This exercise is not to be discussion only, but to plan concrete actions. (For example, if six- to eight-year-olds pick pollution, then careful recycling at home or picking up litter around the church are both concrete actions.) Although the groups are looking at only one problem, they can list as many solutions as possible.

When everyone is finished, share these lists and show off the preschool drawings. Then ask everyone to return to their families for the Closing Ritual.

Closing Ritual. If miracles are to continue today, we are called by Jesus to join him as miracle workers. Have each family begin this ritual by deciding which concrete action they will start tomorrow. Then darken the room as much as possible. Have a member of each family come forward and light one of the vigil candles on the prayer table. (If your group is small, it may be more effective to have each member of the family light a vigil candle.) Notice how much brighter even these few candles make the darkness.

Lead them in this prayer:

"Jesus, you performed many miracles while you lived here on earth. We still need you today to heal us and make us whole. Help us to remember that we need each other as well, that we are called to be your eyes, your hands and your voice in our world. Teach us to be miracle workers joined with you in love. Amen."

Dismissal. Remind everyone to read "Bartimaeus" and "The Special Picnic" and to complete the activity pages for these stories before the next gathering.

'The Last Days of Jesus'

Materials Needed: *Jesus Lives*, nametags, instrumental music, crosses cut out of poster board, candle, Bible, crucifix, paper, pencils and crayons.

Schedule *(90 minutes):*
- Welcome, Set the Environment
  (10 minutes)
- Opening Activity *(5 minutes)*
- Getting Started *(15 minutes)*
- Read the Story *(10 minutes)*
- Discuss the Story *(10 minutes)*
- Together Time Activity *(30 minutes)*
- Closing Ritual *(10 minutes)*

Objectives: To review Jesus' life by remembering favorite stories about Jesus.
  To recognize that Jesus had enemies who wanted to stop the Good News.

Theme: Jesus' life was an example to us: He lived the Good News all through his life, even to his death.

Background for Program Leaders:

1) Read "The Last Days of Jesus" in both Storybooks.
2) Read the commentary, Theme and Optional Activities for "The Last Days of Jesus" on the Grown-up's Pages in the Activity Books.

3) This session is a tough one in many ways, since it deals with the passion and death of Jesus. But it is also the source of our understanding of the Eucharist and of our salvation. It will be mostly prayerful reflection, and you will need to judge how best to encourage this for your gathering.

Set the Environment. Welcome all the participants and ask them to wear nametags. Ask some of the families to help you set up a prayer table with a candle, a Bible and a crucifix.

Opening Activity. To maintain a quiet and prayerful mood, invite everyone to sit comfortably in an area around the prayer table. Have quiet instrumental or classical music playing in the background.

Getting Started. Have each family discuss: If you could live over one day in your life, what day would it be? Why?

Read the Story. Have the families read the material appropriate to the ages of their young people.

Discuss the Story. Staying in the family groups, discuss the material shared.
1) Do you have any questions about this reading?
2) Why do you think people wanted to get rid of Jesus?
3) Jesus knew his enemies were in Jerusalem. Why do you think he went there anyway?

Together Time Activity. Give each family a cross made of poster board. Have them sit quietly with their eyes shut as you lead them through this meditation with soft music in the background. Pause about twenty seconds between phrases. This is meant to be slow and deliberate. People need time to create the images you suggest.

> "Breath deeply and slowly. Feel the air go into your body and come out through your mouth.
>
> "Imagine yourself walking down a path in a lush green forest. You come to a small bench in a sunny spot and sit down. As you look down the path you see a woman walking toward you. This woman is Mary, the mother of Jesus. Greet her any way you wish.
>
> "Mary has come to share her favorite memory of Jesus with you. Sit with her on the bench and listen as she speaks to you. This memory may be happy or sad, but it is meant just for you." (*At this point, take a few minutes of silence.*)
>
> "Now it is your turn. Tell Mary your favorite memory of Jesus. Think back over all the stories, the friendships and miracles you have learned about this year. What do you want to tell Mary?" (*Again allow a few minutes of silence.*)
>
> "Open your hand and hold it out to Mary. Imagine she places a gift in your hand. What is it?
>
> "When you are finished, leave Mary and walk back down the path of the forest. When you are ready, open your eyes."

After this guided meditation, ask each family to fill in the cross in front of them with words, drawings, images or phrases that came to them during this meditation, and the gift they received from Mary. Have them bring the crosses with them to the Closing Ritual.

Closing Ritual. Place the crosses in front of each family as you sit in a circle (this means the crosses will be in the center of the circle). Have everyone raise their right hands over the crosses. Ask everyone to join you silently in blessing these crosses as you pray:

> "Jesus, we know you have asked us to remember you. We remember your life and your death. We remember your joy and your sorrow. Most of all, we remember how you loved us, how you love us now and how we love you. Bless these crosses of memory and bless all of us who take them to our homes today. We ask this of God through the Holy Spirit. Amen."

Ask each family to keep the cross in a place of honor at home until you gather again. End with the Our Father.

Dismissal. Remind everyone to read "Arriving in Jerusalem" and "How Jesus Died" and to complete the activity pages for these stories before the next gathering.

'Jesus Is Alive'

Materials Needed: *Jesus Lives*, nametags, the prayer table symbols for the year, slips of paper, candle, Bible, pencils and crayons.

Schedule *(90 minutes)*:
- Welcome, Set the Environment
  (10 minutes)
- Opening Activity/Getting Started
  (25 minutes)
- Read the Story *(10 minutes)*
- Discuss the Story *(10 minutes)*
- Together Time Activity *(30 minutes)*
- Closing Ritual *(5 minutes)*

Objectives: To recognize that Jesus is still alive with us today.

To affirm how we are "Jesus" for each other.

Theme: Even death had no power over Jesus. He is alive and with us today.

Background for Program Leaders:

1) Read "Jesus Is Alive" in Storybooks.
2) Read the commentary, Theme and Optional Activities for "Jesus Is Alive" on the Grown-up's Pages in the Activity Books.
3) This is the most joyous session, the Resurrection of Jesus! This is the central message of our Christian faith: Jesus has defeated death and sin for us forever! Spend some time preparing for this

gathering by thinking about what Easter means for you. Are you able to sing Alleluia with your whole heart? If not, what is stopping you?

Set the Environment. Welcome all the participants and ask them to wear nametags. Ask some of the families to help you set up a prayer table with a candle, a Bible and all the symbols you have used throughout this year's sessions.

Opening Activity/Getting Started. As the participants arrive, have them take a small slip of paper and write down the answer to "What was one (or two) of the happiest times of your life?" Children too young to write can have an adult fill out their slip for them, but that adult must be very quiet during the activity and not give away the child's identity. *No one else should know what anyone has written.* Fold the slips and place them in a paper bag.

As you begin the session, point out: "This is our last session together. We have learned much about Jesus, but I hope we have also learned much about each other as well." Then pass the bag around the group and have each person draw a slip of paper. (If you draw your own, put it back!) Again, adults can assist children too young to read. Then each person must try to guess whose slip of paper they have drawn.

Read the Story. Have each family read the age-appropriate material.

Discuss the Story. Break into mixed-generation groups and discuss the material shared.

1) What was your favorite part of the story?
2) When the women who found the empty tomb were older, what do you think they told their grandchildren about Jesus?
3) How do you think you can share the Good News as Jesus did?

Together Time Activity. Staying in the mixed-generation groups, have each member of the group name one person who has been "Jesus" for him or her. This should be someone the child or adult actually knows or knew in the past (as opposed to a public figure or saint). Discuss why these people were representatives of the risen Jesus for you.

Then give each person a piece of pastel construction paper. In the middle of the paper, each person should write his or her name (or have an adult write it). Then the participant should pass the paper to the immediate right. Each member of the group writes around the person's name some way that he or she has been "Jesus" for the intergenerational program.

By the time the construction paper returns to the hands of the sender, every member of the group should have written some affirming comment. This is how we are "alleluia" moments for each other.

Closing Ritual. The Closing Ritual should blend right into the preceding activity. After you give people a few minutes to read what has been written, ask them to rejoin their families. Sing together an Alleluia used in your community's Sunday liturgies. Read aloud (preferably from a children's lectionary or Bible) one of the Gospel accounts of Jesus' Resurrection. Say the Our Father together for all your intentions and offer each other a Sign of Peace.

Dismissal. Remind everyone to read the "Jesus Is Alive" optional activities. Ask them to continue praying for each other over the time they are apart. Thank them for a great year together.

Year Three: *Spirit With Us*

'Pentecost:
The Day the Spirit Came'

Materials Needed: *Spirit With Us*, storybooks, banner with flame and "SPIRIT WITH US" already drawn on it (see page 68), permanent markers, fabric paint, nametags, candle, Bible, blackboard or flip chart, paper, pencils and crayons.

Schedule *(90 minutes)*:
- Welcome, Set the Environment *(10 minutes)*
- Opening Activity *(20 minutes)*
- Getting Started *(10 minutes)*
- Read the Story *(5 minutes)*
- Discuss the Story *(10 minutes)*
- Together Time Activity *(25 minutes)*
- Closing Ritual *(10 minutes)*

Objectives: To explain why Pentecost is considered the "birthday" of the Church.

To identify the action of the Holy Spirit in our personal history as well as in our communal history.

Theme: The Reign of God happens whenever we live with love for God and others. The Spirit of God is with us and great things happen when we are open to the Spirit.

Background for Program Leaders:

1) Read "The Spirit at Work" and "Pentecost: The Day the Spirit Came" in both Storybooks.
2) Read the commentary, Theme and Optional Activities for "The Spirit at Work" and "Pentecost: The Day the Spirit Came" on the Grown-up's Pages in the Activity Books.
3) The role of the Holy Spirit in our Church is important, but sometimes difficult to grasp. Think about what the word *spirit* has meant in your experiences and find ways to connect those insights with the Holy Spirit. (For example, a "spirited discussion" means both parties care deeply about the topic. Caring deeply is a sign of the Spirit as well.)

Set the Environment. Since this is the first session of the year, be sure to welcome all the participants and ask them to wear nametags. Ask some of the families to help you set up a prayer table with a candle, a Bible and any other symbol you want. (An artistic representation or symbol of the Holy Spirit would be especially appropriate for this gathering.) If possible, have some quiet instrumental or classical music playing in the background.

Opening Activity. It is important that people begin by learning each other's names. Play some type of game to help people begin associating names and faces.

One option that works well with younger children is using the first initial of the name to identify a hobby or interest, for example, "I am Mary and I like watching movies." Every one repeats after the person, "You are Mary and you like watching movies." Then go around again and have each person say only his or her first name. Everyone else has to try to remember what hobby or interest the person named.

Getting Started. Have each family discuss: Who are some of the people you love? How do you show your love? How do they show their love to you?

Read the Story. Divide the children into age-level groups (preschool and first grade, ages seven through ten, ages eleven through fourteen). Teenagers and adults should sit with each of the groups to assist them. (Teens often enjoy leading younger groups.) Read the material appropriate to the ages of the young people. The younger children will need to be read to; older children may wish to read the section to themselves.

Discuss the Story. Staying in the age-level groups, discuss the material shared.
  1) What do we mean when we talk about the Plan or Reign of God?
  2) Who are the three Persons in the Holy Trinity? How do we see God acting in three ways today?

Together Time Activity. It is important to spend time at the first session each year to establish a covenant with the participants. Recording their answers on a flip chart or blackboard, ask everyone what is needed to make these family gatherings successful. (Some examples: Participate with an open mind, attend meetings faithfully, listen to each other and so on.) Be sure you list what you and other catechists or leaders are also willing to do (provide supplies, prepare material and so on). Then prepare a banner that you will use all year to symbolize your community and this covenant. Bring out the fabric on which you have already drawn a large flame and written "SPIRIT WITH US" with paint or permanent marker. On the edges of the flame, have each participant write (or get an adult to write) his or her name in marking pen. Writing the names on the flame is a sign of agreement to the covenant.

Closing Ritual. Place the Bible reverently on the table. Tell the participants that all the stories they will be reading are found in this holy book. Lift up the Bible with both hands and offer a prayer of thanks:

> "We thank you, God, for the word you have given us. We ask to be open to the teachings of the stories contained here and to the teachings of the stories of our lives. Be with us through this year as we listen for your call. We ask this in confidence through Jesus and your Holy Spirit. Amen."

End with the Sign of the Cross.

Dismissal. Remind everyone to read "The Spirit at Work" and "Pentecost: The Day the Spirit Came" and to complete the activity pages for these stories before the next gathering.

If your budget allows, purchase white T-shirts for each participant for the next session. If that is not possible, ask each participant to bring in a T-shirt for the next session. (Any T-shirt will do as long as at least one side of the shirt is blank.)

Spirit With Us

'Spirit of Belonging'

Materials Needed: *Spirit With Us*, nametags, T-shirts (either purchased or brought from home by participants), permanent markers or fabric pens, candle, pitcher, bowl, Bible, paper, pencils and crayons.

Schedule *(90 minutes)*:
- Welcome, Set the Environment *(10 minutes)*
- Opening Activity *(25 minutes)*
- Getting Started *(5 minutes)*
- Read the Story *(5 minutes)*
- Discuss the Story *(5 minutes)*
- Together Time Activity *(30 minutes)*
- Closing Ritual *(10 minutes)*

Objectives: To introduce the Sacrament of Baptism as initiation into the Catholic Church.

To discuss how we, as Church, welcome and include each other into our community.

Theme: The Sacrament of Baptism makes us members of the Church family, the Catholic community.

Background for Program Leaders:

1) Read the "Spirit of Belonging" in both Storybooks.
2) Read the commentary, Theme, and Optional Activities for "Spirit of Belonging" on the Grown-up's Pages in the Activity Books.

3) The drive to "belong" is strong in our human family. Where do you feel that you belong? Is your church community a safe haven for you? Can you share that with the families in your program?

Set the Environment. Welcome all the participants and ask them to wear nametags. Ask some of the families to help you set up a prayer table with a candle, a Bible, a pitcher of water and an empty bowl.

Opening Activity. The first group we belong to is our family. (Remember that, in this program, *family* is the name for whatever configuration of adults and children are coming to your program. You don't decide what the word means to them; they do.) In family groups, have each family identify a symbol for themselves in something they brought with them to this session. It can be something from a pocket, purse or wallet, or an article of clothing or jewelry. It can be anything as long as one family member has it on his or her person.

Each family then comes forward and explains their symbol.

Getting Started. Have each family discuss: When was the last time you felt truly appreciated or accepted? What happened as a result?

Read the Story. In family groups, read the material appropriate to the ages of the young people. Younger children will need to be read to; older children may wish to read the section to themselves.

Discuss the Story. Divide into mixed-generation groups. (Count off young people first, then adults. Preschool children may wish to stay with particular adults and should not be included in the counting.) Discuss the material shared in these small groups.

1) When are you most likely to feel lonely? Why?
2) When are you most likely to feel accepted and wanted? Why?
3) How do you make someone feel welcome?

Together Time Activity. Each group will need T-shirts and permanent markers or fabric pens.

Ask all participants to name some words that describe how they feel when they know they belong. A member of the group should record these words. Then all name ways they can help others feel they belong. This list is also recorded.

From these lists, each person should pick a word and print it on his or her T-shirt. (An older member can write the chosen word for young children.) The word can also be symbolized by a drawing (smiling face, flower and so on).

Then everyone else in the group should (if asked) be willing to write a word, phrase or symbol of welcome on someone else's T-shirt. Participants may collect as many of these words of welcome as they wish. Groups can mingle with other groups to add more welcoming words. The point is to show that in this intergenerational program, everyone belongs. That is the way we model the Spirit of Belonging!

Closing Ritual. Water is the symbol of Baptism. Pour the water from the pitcher into the bowl saying, "Spirit of God, wash me in love." Have everyone repeat this after you three times. Then invite the participants to come forward and bless themselves with this water and the Sign of the Cross.

Close by saying together this paraphrase of the doxology from the Mass:

> "Through Jesus, in Jesus, and with Jesus, in the unity of the Holy Spirit, all glory and honor is yours, Almighty Father, forever and ever. Amen."

Dismissal. Remind everyone to read "Philip and the Ethiopian" and "The Maiden Who Finally Found a Home" and to complete the activity pages for these stories before the next gathering.

'Spirit of Prayer'

Materials Needed: *Spirit With Us*, nametags, candle, enough Bibles or children's Bibles for each group, clay, grape juice, loaf of bread, paper, pencils and crayons, copies of Prayer Bingo handout (page 73).

Schedule *(90 minutes):*
- Welcome, Set the Environment *(10 minutes)*
- Opening Activity *(10 minutes)*
- Read the Story *(10 minutes)*
- Discuss the Story *(10 minutes)*
- Together Time Activity *(30 minutes)*
- Closing Ritual *(20 minutes)*

Objectives: To introduce the Sacrament of the Eucharist as the primary source of our continuing relationship with our God.

To use Jesus as our model of the need for consistent personal prayer.

Theme: There are many different ways to spend time with God in prayer. The Eucharist nourishes our relationship with God.

Background for Program Leaders:

1) Read "Spirit of Prayer" in both Storybooks.
2) Read the commentary, Theme and Optional Activities for "Spirit of Prayer" on the Grown-up's Pages in the Activity Books.

3) This session will be spent mostly in a prayer experience. All prayer is important to our relationship with God and God's Spirit, but the highest of all our prayers is the Eucharist. Be willing to share your enthusiasm for the Eucharist with the participants.

Set the Environment. Welcome all the participants and ask them to wear nametags. Ask some of the families to help you set up a prayer table with a candle, a Bible, the grape juice in a pitcher or carafe and the loaf of bread.

Opening Activity. Play "prayer bingo" with your group. (See diagram on page 73.) Each participant should try to cover all the boxes with names of other participants who fit the categories. No one may use his or her own name or anyone else's name more than twice (three times if your group is small).

At the end of the time allotted, ask what categories were hard to fill. See which people in the room could have filled in their names.

Getting Started. Have each family discuss: What's the most fun you've had spending time with a friend? Why?

Read the Story. In family groups, read the material appropriate to the ages of the young people.

Discuss the Story. Staying in the family groups, discuss:

1) Is there someplace where it's easier for you to pray? Why?
2) What do you like about praying?

Together Time Activity. Give each participant a small clump of clay. Play quiet music in the background. Lead them through this prayer experience:

"Hold the clay in your hand and work with it until it is soft.

"We are in the hands of our God who takes us from the hardness of our lives, our stony hearts, and gives us soft, living hearts.

"I'm going to read to you from the Bible about times when Jesus prayed. As soon as you hear something that makes you think about how you pray, I want you to form the clay into some type of symbol for yourself. Think of this symbol as a way to show who you really are to God, for when we pray we show our true selves to God.

"Just as we aren't perfect, your symbol doesn't have to be perfect, either!"

Then begin to read the following passages in which Jesus talked about praying or prayed: Matthew 3:13-17; Matthew 6:5-15; Matthew 14:22-24; Mark 1:35-37; Mark 6:41-44; Luke 4:14-21; Luke 6:12-16; Luke 22:39-46; John 17:9-24.

Because you will be passing around bread to eat during the Closing Ritual, allow some time for participants to wash their hands.

Closing Ritual. Have the participants bring their symbols to the prayer circle and place them in front of themselves. Open by praying:

"Spirit of Prayer, you help us bring our hearts, our minds and our whole selves to God in prayer. Jesus taught us that whenever two or more of us gather, you are with us. Jesus also told us to remember him whenever we break bread together and give thanks. Be with us today as we share this bread with thanks for all we have received. Amen."

Then break the loaf of bread in half and pass to either side of you in the circle. As the participants break off a piece of the bread, they may briefly explain their clay symbol, if they wish. Then they consume the bread. If the size of your crowd and the available time allow, you may also wish to pour the grape juice into two glasses and start them around the circle as well. Close with the doxology: "Through Jesus, in Jesus and with Jesus, in the unity of the Holy Spirit, all glory and honor is yours, Almighty Father, forever and ever. Amen."

Dismissal. Remind everyone to read "The Church at Home" and "The Woman Who Laughed With God" and to complete the activity pages for these stories before the next gathering.

Prayer Bingo

Carries a rosary	Knows the Hail Mary	Has owned a missal	Keeps a journal	Says Morning Offering
Plays in nature	Attends daily Mass	Prays before meals	Knows the Our Father	Kneels to pray
Talks to God like a friend	Had a prayer answered	**FREE SPACE**	Has a cross or crucifix	Complains to God
Thinks God has a sense of humor	Uses music in prayer	Likes to pray alone	Likes to pray with others	Thanks God often
Learned to pray at home	Learned to pray at school	Asks God for help	Asks God to forgive	Knows the "Jesus Prayer"

'Spirit of Forgiveness'

Materials Needed: *Spirit With Us*, nametags, ten-inch circles of poster board or heavy construction paper (three for each group), glue, magazines, newspapers, markers, candle, Bible, paper, pencils and crayons.

Schedule *(90 minutes)*:
• Welcome, Set the Environment
  (10 minutes)
• Opening Activity *(15 minutes)*
• Getting Started *(15 minutes)*
• Read the Story *(10 minutes)*
• Discuss the Story *(10 minutes)*
• Together Time Activity *(20 minutes)*
• Closing Ritual *(10 minutes)*

Objectives: To introduce the Sacrament of Reconciliation as the healing celebration of God's forgiveness.

To recognize the need for God's forgiveness by honestly examining personal and social sins (the "circles of hurt").

Theme: The Sacrament of Reconciliation is the Church's celebration of God's mercy and forgiveness.

Background for Program Leaders:

1) Read "Spirit of Forgiveness" in both Storybooks.

2) Read the commentary, Theme, and Optional Activities for "Spirit of Forgiveness" on the Grown-up's Pages in the Activity Books.

3) Our call to forgive others is certainly one of Jesus' clearest messages in the Gospels. It is also one of the hardest things we are ever asked to do. Before you lead this session, spend some time in prayer over a hurt you have not yet forgiven, whether it is someone else or yourself that you can't seem to forgive. Ask God truly to give you the Spirit of forgiveness and set you free.

Set the Environment. Welcome all the participants and ask them to wear nametags. Ask some of the families to help you set up a prayer table with a candle, a Bible and the poster board circles.

Opening Activity. Form mixed-generation groups. Have each group sit in a row on the floor, one behind another, for a type of relay race.

The last person in each line is given a drawing (this should be simple but recognizable—a tree, a sun or a flower, for example.) The first person in each line is given a piece of paper and a pencil.

The last people in line, the only ones who may see the drawing, begin by drawing it with a finger on the backs of the people seated directly in front of them. Those people may ask to have it drawn on their backs more than once until they think they know what it is. They may not guess aloud what the drawing is, but must proceed to draw it on the backs of the people in front of them. This continues down the line, until the first person is able to draw the figure on the piece of paper.

The team coming closest to the original drawing wins.

This game shows how things "ripple out" and change as they move from one person to another. Sin and hurt, as well as forgiveness and healing, ripple out this way as well.

Getting Started. Have each mixed-generation group discuss: When was the last time you had to say "I'm sorry"? When was the last time you had to forgive someone else?

Read the Story. Read the material appropriate to the ages of the young people. Younger children will need to be read to; older children may wish to read to themselves.

Discuss the Story. Staying in the mixed-generation groups, discuss the material shared.

1) How do you feel when you have made a mistake or even hurt someone? What do you do?
2) Are there any people you feel you can't forgive? Why? What would make it possible for you to forgive them?

Together Time Activity. Give each group three poster board circles. Ask them to use magazines and newspapers or their own drawings or phrases and fill the first circle with "the hurts or sins of the world" (pictures of poverty, stories of violence and so on).

When they have finished the first circle, tell them to fill in the second circle with "the hurts or sins of our community." They may again use magazines or newspapers, but the sins in the first circle (the world) should help them focus on local evils as well. (For example, if there is a picture of a war in another country on the world circle, gang fights in your own city would be a local representation of the same evil.)

On the third circle, they need to write how these world and community sins are hurting their families, their friends and themselves. This is the circle of "personal hurts or sins."

When the circles are finished, each group should spend some time discussing how these sins and hurts can be forgiven, changed and healed. Not all of them will have answers, of course, but prayer and forgiveness is where the Good News starts!

Each group also needs to prepare a short prayer based on the sins in their circles. It should begin, "Lord, we are sorry that we...." One person from each group will need to offer that prayer during the Closing Ritual.

Closing Ritual. Open with the Sign of the Cross. Then ask someone to read 2 Corinthians 5:17-19.

Ask a representative from each small group to respond by sharing their "Lord, we are sorry" prayers. After each prayer, the entire gathering should say, "Forgive us, Lord."

Then lead them in this prayer of sorrow:

> "God of loving mercy, we are not perfect people, but we are trying to be your followers. Help us to admit when we do wrong. Lead us to reconcile with others. Guide us to healing the world with your justice and peace. We ask all this through, with and in Jesus and the Holy Spirit. Amen."

Bless yourself and all there by raising your right hand and inviting them to do the same as you say,

> "As you forgive us, Lord, let us forgive others. Bless us and heal us. Amen."

Close by offering each other a Sign of Peace.

Dismissal. Remind everyone to read "The Man Who Made Trouble" and "The Soldier Who Had No Enemies" and to complete the activity pages for these stories before the next gathering.

'Spirit of Action'

Materials Needed: *Spirit With Us*, coffee stirrers, a roll of butcher paper, nametags, candle, Bible, paper, pencils and crayons.

Schedule *(90 minutes):*
- Welcome, Set the Environment
  (5 minutes)
- Opening Activity *(15 minutes)*
- Getting Started *(10 minutes)*
- Read the Story *(10 minutes)*
- Discuss the Story *(10 minutes)*
- Together Time Activity *(30 minutes)*
- Closing Ritual *(10 minutes)*

Objectives: To introduce the Sacrament of Confirmation as strengthening our ability to love as people of involved, committed action.

To discuss ways we can follow Jesus' gospel mandate, relying upon the promised gifts of the Holy Spirit.

Theme: The Sacrament of Confirmation reaffirms our baptismal call to act in establishing the Reign of God.

Background for Program Leaders:

1) Read "Spirit of Action" in both Storybooks.
2) Read the commentary, Theme and Optional Activities for "Spirit of Action" on the Grown-up's Pages in the Activity Books.

3) Sometimes we seem to think that being a Christian is pretty easy and rather passive. Worse, we seem to think that being a Christian is unrelated to our daily lives! This is truly a waste of our gifts, especially the gifts we have received from the Spirit through Confirmation. Identify some daily actions in your life that are directly related to your faith in Jesus. Are there any new actions you should be considering?

Set the Environment. Welcome all the participants and ask them to wear nametags. Ask some of the families to help you set up a prayer table with a candle, a Bible and some symbol of wind (a wind chime or a mobile, perhaps, or a wind instrument—a flute, a tin whistle).

Opening Activity. Give each family fifteen to twenty coffee stirrers. Ask them to try to make a structure that can stand up on its own. After a few minutes, have them join with another family. Then after a few minutes more, have those two families join with two other families. Eventually, all will be working on one structure. By the time you get all the coffee stirrers in one spot, building a solid structure should be no problem.

Point out how easy it is to rip one page of the phone book, and how difficult to rip the entire phone book. "We" are definitely stronger than "I."

Getting Started. Have each family discuss: When have you surprised or embarrassed yourself by the way you were acting? What was going on? How did you feel later?

Read the Story. Read the material appropriate to the ages of the young people. Younger children will need to be read to; older children may wish to read to themselves.

Discuss the Story. In family groups, discuss the material shared:
1) Do you try to say what you mean and do what you say? Give an example.
2) Are there times when you think people are telling you one thing but doing something very different? (This is called hypocrisy.) How does this make you feel?

Together Time Activity. Break into mixed-generation groups. Have one of the smaller children lie down on a long piece of butcher paper. Have one of the older children carefully outline this child on the paper.

Then discuss how Jesus wants us to be his hands, his eyes, his lips, his feet and his heart. In other words, list how your group sees the world (eyes), what it tells others about Jesus (lips), what it holds onto and what it gives away (hands), where you all are willing to go (feet), and how you show love (heart).

After this discussion, finish drawing your outlined Christian. Be sure to find a way to represent how we must be Jesus in the world.

Closing Ritual. In family groups, make the Sign of the Cross on each other's hands, eyes and lips. As you make these three signs of blessing on each other, say,

"Through Jesus *[bless hands]*, with Jesus *[bless eyes]*, and in Jesus *[bless lips]*, in the unity of the Holy Spirit, all glory and honor is yours, Almighty Father, forever and ever. Amen."

Dismissal. Remind everyone to read "A Letter of Good News" and "The Bishop for the Poor" and to complete the activity pages for these stories before the next gathering.

'The Not-the-End'

> **Materials Needed:** *Spirit With Us*, nametags, candle, Bible, paper, pencils and crayons.
>
> **Schedule** *(90 minutes):*
> - Welcome, Set the Environment
>   *(10 minutes)*
> - Opening Activity *(15 minutes)*
> - Getting Started *(15 minutes)*
> - Read the Story *(10 minutes)*
> - Discuss the Story *(10 minutes)*
> - Together Time Activity *(20 minutes)*
> - Closing Ritual *(10 minutes)*
>
> **Objectives:** To review how the stories in *Spirit With Us* can provide models and insights for our personal lives and for the life of our Church.
>
> To reflect on how the Holy Spirit continues to be alive in our stories and our actions today.
>
> **Theme:** Individually and in community, we are sacraments because we continue to show the Spirit of God in our actions and our lives.

Background for Program Leaders:

1) Read "The Not-the-End" in both Storybooks.
2) Read the commentary, Theme and Optional Activities for "The Not-the-End" on the Grown-up's Pages in the Activity Books.

3) This is the last session for this year. Where do you feel you are in your story? Where is God acting in your life as director of this program? Can you share this with the families in your program?

Set the Environment. Welcome all the participants and ask them to wear nametags. Ask some of the families to help you set up a prayer table with a candle, a Bible and all the symbols you used during the year's sessions.

Opening Activity. Prepare signs (typing paper will do) with the names Philip, Kateri Tekakwitha, Nympha, Thea Bowman, Paul, Maximilian Kolbe, James and Oscar Romero. Hang these signs in various areas in the room or place them on different tables.

To form your groups for the evening, ask people to go to the person whose story they liked best. If any group is especially large, you can break it into smaller groups. Six is probably the maximum number for this activity.

Have each group prepare three questions (a "trivia challenge") about the person they chose. Collect all the questions for the Together Time Activity.

Getting Started. Have each group discuss: Who is the best storyteller in your family or among your friends? Why?

Read the Story. Read the material appropriate to the ages of the young people.

Discuss the Story. Staying in the same groups, discuss:
1) Do you believe your story is the most important one in the book?
Why or why not?
2) Why was the person whose story you chose your favorite?

Together Time Activity. The last chapter of *Spirit With Us* has space for the children to write their own stories. But this is an individual activity, not a group activity. This closing activity is meant to review the insights gained during the year.

Have your groups ready to play the "Trivia Challenge" for which they wrote questions during the Opening Activity. Read the questions and allow each group a chance to answer in rotation. (Of course, the "Oscar Romero" group won't be asked its own questions, and so forth.) You may want to have some questions of your own ready to go. Each right answer is worth a point, and the team with the most points at the end is the "Spirit-wise" team.

Closing Ritual. Since this is your last session, it would be nice to share a meal together. If that's not possible, at least arrange a special snack.

Before you begin to eat, offer this prayer:

"Spirit of God, Spirit with us, you are our true nourishment. We thank you for giving us a place to belong, the desire to pray, the courage to forgive and the wisdom to act. Keep in your love the poor, the ill, the oppressed and the lonely. And bring us all together as we work towards God's Reign. We ask this through Jesus, with Jesus, and in Jesus, in the unity of the Holy Spirit, now and forever. Amen."

Dismissal. Remind the participants to write their "Not-the-End" stories at home.

Part Three

Initiating Children
of Catechetical Age

An Overview of the Process

The process of becoming a member of the Church involves stages or "steps marking the catechumens' progress, as they pass, so to speak, through another doorway or ascend to the next level" (*Rite of Christian Initiation of Adults*, #6).

Precatechumenate

This is a period of pre-evangelization and evangelization, a time to build trust, tell stories and begin hearing the Good News. It involves the following components of the series:

- Opening retreat ("Sharing Stories")
- Monthly meetings with other families
- Reading and reflecting on Scripture as a family at home

Catechumenate

This period is a time of continued evangelization, a time of budding faith, the beginning of conversion, a continuation of the proclamation. It involves the following components:

- Continue monthly meeting with family groups
- Advent Retreat (salvation history until the time of Christ)
- Rite of Becoming a Catechumen
- Presentation of the Creed and Our Father
- Continue reading and reflecting on Scripture at home with family members

Purification and Enlightenment

This period just prior to the sacraments of initiation is a time for preparation, recollection and prayer. The following components are part of this important stage:

- Enrollment of Names
- A retreat to reflect on who Jesus is
- Penitential Rite for Families
- Another retreat focusing on signs, symbols and sacrament
- No other monthly gatherings

Mystagogia

This period, which follows the sacraments of initiation, is a time of celebration. It is also a time to talk about and process the experience of the Rite of Christian Initiation. It involves the following components:

- Monthly meetings
- Time for sharing the experience
- Encouraging families to continue growing in their faith by becoming regular members of the Family Group

Children's Catechumenate and Catch-up Catechesis

There are two essential factors to remember when inviting children of catechetical age to become members of our Church: (1) The process must always be relevant to the ages of the children involved (see *RCIA* #307). (2) It is important that the children's parents, as well as peers who have already been baptized, are involved in the process (see *RCIA* #308). These factors also apply when we welcome young people back to the Church. The "God Is Calling" series meets both of these needs.

The materials found in the Storybooks and Activity Books, along with the pages that follow, offer a comprehensive approach to the process of catechesis and initiation. If your parish is using the series as an ongoing family catechetical program, the family presenting a child for Baptism is simply invited to join the gatherings. If you would like to use the series solely for children's catechumenate and/or catch-up catechesis, you will find an alternate schedule in the Overview of the Series, page 11.

It is important to emphasize, however, that the materials in this series are only one component in the whole process of initiating children into our faith. This series is not to be seen as a total catechetical package. The Rite itself, as well as the lectionary, provides the foundation on which any additional process rests. (For example, if adults are being dismissed from Mass following the reading of the Gospel, it is appropriate that children are also dismissed to break open the word of God.) Those who are facilitating the process must be well versed in the Rite of Christian Initiation of Adults, particularly Chapter Five, which deals with unbaptized children of catechetical age. Any necessary adaptations for children will be found there. If no changes are indicated, use the adult rite.

Remember throughout the process to distinguish between children who are being baptized and children who are being received into the Church. You might want to mention at one of the first meetings that as Catholics we believe in one Baptism. Therefore, anyone who has already been baptized in another faith does not need to be baptized again.

Adapting the Series for Children's Catechumenate

When using this series for children who are to be baptized or are returning to the faith, the facilitator needs to take care of two additional matters: (1) Invite specific sponsoring families to become a part of the gatherings and (2) adjust meeting schedules, as well as some meeting contents.

Sponsoring Families. Make sure there is a particular family that agrees to mentor each family that is presenting children for Baptism. As mentors they will be part of as many gatherings as possible, take the initiative in welcoming the new family, spend some time socializing with the family during break times, introduce them to other parish members and be available to listen and encourage. Often a family is attracted to the Church because of friends or neighbors who have invited them to "come and see." If this is the case, that family may be an appropriate sponsoring family. If this is not the situation, look at families who are already a part of the family group or go through the parish roster. In either case try to find a sponsoring family that includes children the same ages as the children who are being initiated. A sponsoring family and age-appropriate peer groups are also important when working with children who have been baptized but not catechized.

Adjusting Schedules. When the families of children in the catechumenate are part of the family gatherings, the three-year calendar will need to be adjusted. If the sacraments of initiation are to be received at Easter, you should not hold meetings during Lent; plan two retreats and a penitential rite or scrutiny instead. The retreat gatherings are about an hour longer than the usual family parish meetings. If possible, serve a pot-luck supper or luncheon. Invite sponsoring families along with any other interested families from the parish to take part in these events. Also, give families (particularly those who will not be meeting) some printed or video materials that offer prayers and ideas on how to celebrate Lent.

Adjust regularly scheduled family gatherings to accommodate the presentation of the Creed and the Our Father. In addition, while the Rite of Acceptance Into the Order of Catechumens is better celebrated with all catechumens, in some cases you may want to celebrate it as part of a regular family gathering. Sometimes a smaller setting is more comfortable for children (*RCIA* #260). Even if the children and their parents celebrate this rite with the larger parish, it is certainly appropriate that they also be recognized within their smaller faith group. The same holds true for the Enrollment of Names. Make sure the pastor and other staff members are asked to be a part of these significant gatherings.

It is important to emphasize that initiating children into our faith is a process that cannot be controlled or contained in a schedule-bound program. There always remains a need for direct personal contact with the individual, to listen and encourage and to help discern readiness. Therefore, you need to remain flexible, adapting the materials, ideas and timetables in the activity books or this guide. With children in the catechumenate, the primary schedule to follow is that of the *Rite of Christian Initiation of Adults*.

Precatechumenate. This initial period is a time of pre-evangelization and evangelization. It is time for those gathered to get to know each other. It is crucial that an atmosphere of trust and confidentiality be established so that the participants feel comfortable and secure. The opening retreat, "Sharing Stories," offers those gathered an opportunity to get in touch with their own family stories as well as with God's story in Scripture. Families meet each other in a warm environment and are encouraged to share their stories with each other at a comfortable level. They are introduced to the concept of "covenant" and asked to consider entering into such an agreement with the group.

Catechumenate. This time begins with the Rite of Acceptance. Following the rite or at the first regular meeting, consider presenting the catechumens with a cross and a Bible as a sign of welcome and encouragement. You may also present either or both of these signs of our faith to the other families who will be a part of the regular gatherings (perhaps one to a family).

During this time families continue to learn more about themselves and each other, about God and the faith. A retreat day at the beginning of Advent celebrates salvation history up until the time of Jesus' birth. Advent is an appropriate time to present the Creed and the Our Father to the catechumens. Do this during one of the regular gatherings, after the adults have been given the appropriate handout with which to prepare their youngsters. Materials to facilitate these presentations can be found in the Appendix.

Purification and Enlightenment. If the sacraments of initiation are celebrated at Easter, this stage of the process coincides with Lent and begins with the Rite of Election or Enrollment of Names. It is important to celebrate the occasion with the family group, whether or not the actual Enrollment of Names takes place during group time. Two retreats are scheduled during Lent.

The first, "Jesus Day," celebrates who Jesus is, why he came and the significance of his death and resurrection. The second retreat, "Signs, Symbols and Sacraments," explores the mission of the Church and the role of the sacraments in that mission. It introduces the elect to the sacraments of initiation, Baptism, Confirmation and Eucharist, along with their corresponding symbols: water, oil and bread.

Also in the Appendix is a suggested reading and response for the celebration of a penitential rite. The Rite calls for at least one such scrutiny with children (*RCIA* #294). You or another staff member may also choose to spend additional time with the young people and/or the adults individually or in peer groups to discuss the sacraments of initation and the details of the ceremony, giving them an opportunity to ask questions.

Mystagogia. This last stage of the initiation process should be marked with all the celebration appropriate for welcoming a sister or brother into the family. It is especially important to gather all of the families within a week or two after initiation to process the experience. Make sure that during the large group gatherings, the families—adults and children together—have time to share their thoughts and feelings about their experience of the Rite. Encourage children's participation and initiate discussion by giving them paper on which to draw their favorite part of the Rite.

The last story and corresponding group activity should be scheduled after the sacraments have been received. If Easter occurs exceptionally early, other stories may also be scheduled later in the Easter Season.

Another Approach to the Catechumenate

If you are not using "God Is Calling" as an ongoing parish family program, you may wish to intensify the initiation process by going through all three Storybooks in one year. You would cover *Yahweh Calls* before Christmas, *Jesus Lives* before Lent (possibly covering the last two stories "Jesus' Last Days" and "Jesus Lives" during the season, and dropping the "Jesus Day" retreat) and *Spirit With Us* during Mystagogia.

This format requires meeting every two weeks during those time periods. Make sure that you invite a few additional families to be part of the process along with the mentoring families. The rest of the process remains the same.

The Presentation of the Our Father and the Creed

Determine an appropriate time during the catechumenate to present these two great prayers to those who are preparing for Baptism or full communion with the Church—possibly during two separate regular parish family gatherings. Following the ritual, present a copy of each prayer to the young person or to the family. You might find a copy suitable for framing or a copy of the prayer on a bookmark or holy card. Date it so that the children can keep it as a memento of the occasion. Remember, however, the presentation of the prayer occurs when the community recites the prayer together, not when the memento is given.

Explain to families of those who are asking for Baptism or full communion the significance of these two prayers. The Our Father is the very prayer Jesus gave his disciples. When the early Church was being persecuted, the Our Father was a secret prayer taught only to Christians or soon-to-be Christians. The Creed is a declaration of all we believe in.

Make copies of the handouts on the next page. Make sure you give the adults adequate instruction: Ask them to go over the page with their youngsters in the time ahead. You may suggest that the children memorize the Our Father.

They should also practice reading the page out loud. Adults read the left side and the children respond by reading the right. Read the first two lines to demonstrate. Tell them that the next time the family group meets, they will join with the other families, adults and children, to read the page together. (Adults will say, "Our Father." Children will respond with, "Our God, you are the source....")

The Our Father

Adults:	**Children:**
Our Father,	Our God, you are the source of all life. You loved us into being. You are the best parent I could ever imagine.
who art in heaven,	We know that your heaven is not just up in the sky. We know it is everywhere because you are everywhere—always loving, always ready to take care of me.
hallowed be thy name;	You are holy; you are all that is sacred. May all people become aware of who you are. And may they honor you by whatever name they know you.
thy kingdom come;	Your Kingdom is both already here and yet to come. The Kingdom is your dream of peace and harmony, of reconciliation and love.
thy will be done on earth as it is in heaven.	Help us to make your dream come true. Help us to be people of peace, harmony and reconciliation. Help us to live in your love.
Give us this day our daily bread;	We ask you to take care of us. Give us what we need for today. And please open our eyes to those in need, so that we can share what we have with them.
and forgive us our trespasses	We have not always lived out your plan of peace and harmony, reconciliation and love. We are sorry. We ask you to forgive us.
as we forgive those who trespass against us;	Because you so lovingly forgive our wrongdoings and our sins, we promise to do our best to forgive those who hurt or wrong us.
and lead us not into temptation, but deliver us from evil.	Protect us from anyone or anything that sets out to harm us. Give us the strength to turn away from wrong and choose the path that leads to you and to all good things.
For the kingdom, the power, and the glory are yours, now and for ever.	Our God, you will always be the greatest. No one is stronger, wiser, more powerful. I am glad you are our God. I am glad that you are my God.
Amen.	I believe! Yes! Yes! I believe!

The Creed

Adults:

We believe in one God,
    the Father, the Almighty,
    maker of heaven and earth,
    of all that is seen and all that is unseen.

We believe in one Lord, Jesus Christ,
    the only Son of God,
    eternally begotten of the Father,
    God from God, Light from Light,
    true God from true God,
    begotten not made, one in Being
      with the Father.
    Through him all things were made.
    For us all and for our salvation
    he came down from heaven:

by the power of the Holy Spirit
    he was born of the Virgin Mary,
      and became man.

For our sake he was crucified under Pontius Pilate;
    he suffered, died, and was buried.
    On the third day he rose again
      in fulfillment of the Scriptures;
    he ascended into heaven
      and is seated at the right hand of the Father.
He will come again in glory to judge the living
      and the dead,
    and his kingdom will have no end.

We believe in the Holy Spirit, the Lord,
    the giver of life,
    who proceeds from the Father and the Son.
    With the Father and the Son he is worshiped
      and glorified.
    He has spoken through the Prophets.
    We believe in one holy catholic
      and apostolic Church.
    We acknowledge one baptism for the
      forgiveness of sins.
    We look for the resurrection of the dead,
      and the life of the world to come.

Amen.

Children:

We believe in God who is the Creator of all things—things that we can see, like trees and water, animals and people. And God is the Creator of things we cannot see, like love and forgiveness, peace and joy.

We believe in Jesus who was born the Son of God and the son of Mary. He did great things. He shouted the Good News that the Reign of God had begun. God's plan was happening. He reconciled and brought comfort. But he was crucified. He died and was buried. Yet the stone that blocked his tomb could not hold him back. Even death had no power over Jesus. And the third day after he died, he rose from the dead. He visited his friends and then went to heaven to sit at the right hand of God. And we believe that someday Jesus will come again.

We believe in the Holy Spirit, who comes from the Father and the Son. The Spirit gives life and shares God's power with us. Long ago the prophets told us about the Spirit, and today we know it is the Spirit who keeps our Church together and holy and always reaching out to all people. We believe in the gift of the Spirit in Baptism, where our sins are forgiven. We worship the Father and the Son and the Spirit as we wait for the resurrection of the dead and life that will last forever.

I believe! Yes! Yes! I believe!

A Penitential Rite With Families

The words and format for this rite, which is similar to the scrutinies celebrated with adult catechumens, can be found in the Rite of Christian Initiation of Adults, #334-342. Below is a reading for use with families.

> "A reading from the book of the prophet Micah.
>
> "And what does the Lord require of you but to do justice, and to love kindness, and to walk humbly with your God?
>
> "The word of the Lord."

Response: "Thanks to you, Lord Jesus Christ."

Print the above reading (Micah 6:8) in large letters on newsprint and place it where everyone can see it. Divide into small groups: family groups, peer groups or intergenerational groups. (By this time you should have a good idea of what will work best.) Give each group a piece of newsprint that has one of the following phrases written on it: "DO JUSTICE"; "LOVE KINDNESS"; "WALK HUMBLY." Tell the groups to spend some time talking about what they think their part of the reading means. After a minute or two ask them to think of all the ways they see this command not lived out in the world. Suggest they look first at their own experiences at home, school or work, then at the larger community and finally at the world and list what they come up with on the newsprint.

Ask them all to share their responses. Hang up the newsprint and ask them to take some quiet time to read what is on the newsprint, reflect on their own lives and examine their own consciences in regard to what they have read.

You may choose either to have them write their own prayers or use the prayer offered below, asking a different person to read each paragraph.

Prayers of Intercession

Response: ("Lord, hear our prayer.")

"We ask God's help to do justice toward the people we meet at work, at school and in our homes; we pray to the Lord.

"We ask God's help to do justice towards those within our own community, throughout the country and the world; we pray to the Lord.

"We ask God's help to do justice in relationship to the environment, in regard to resources, food, water, and so on; we pray to the Lord.

"We ask God's help to love kindness, to be kind to those closest to us, our family and friends; we pray to the Lord.

"We ask God's help to love kindness, to be kind to those whom we know casually, at work, at school or in other social situations; we pray to the Lord.

"We ask God's help to love kindness, to be kind to those people who most need our love; we pray to the Lord.

"We ask for help to walk humbly with our God, to spend time with God; we pray to the Lord.

"We ask for help to walk humbly with our God, to get to know God better through study or in community; we pray to the Lord.

"We ask for help to walk humbly with our God, to see Jesus in others and treat everyone as we would treat him; we pray to the Lord.

"This is what God asks of us, only this: to do justice, to love kindness and to walk humbly with our God."

Part Four

Family Retreats

Sharing Stories Retreat

This opening retreat introduces families and other interested individuals to "God Is Calling," a series of parish gatherings structured to nurture and encourage faith sharing. The retreat begins with an icebreaker that requires participants to work together to "unravel" themselves as they learn three important lessons: to pause and take stock, to work together and to listen to each other.

The first activity, "Family Memories," gives families a chance to sit together and talk about significant family moments. They are then asked to gather with the large group to introduce themselves and share as much as they like about memories.

Following a break and another icebreaker, participants divide into groups to put together a puzzle. When all four corners of the puzzle are put together, participants realize that the puzzle is still incomplete. After a brief discussion on how the unfinished puzzles are like our understanding of God, families regather to learn how to find more pieces to the "God puzzle."

Each family receives a Scripture citation to find and read during the Closing Prayer. This prayer focuses on the concept of covenant, and the participants are invited to make their own covenant.

Schedule (150 minutes):
- "Unraveling"
    (large group, 15 minutes)
- "Family Memories"
    (family groups, 20 minutes)
- "Sharing Stories"
    (large group, 35 minutes)
- Break (10 minutes)
- "Big Shoes/Little Shoes"
    (forming intergenerational groups
    of four, 10 minutes)
- "Puzzle Solvers"
    (intergenerational groups, 15 minutes)
- "God Is a Puzzle"
    (large group, 10 minutes)
- "Scripture Passages"
    (family groups, 20 minutes)
- Closing Prayer (large group, 15 minutes)

Materials Needed: Bibles, pencils, a copy of the Handout Page "Family Stories" (page 97) for each family, newsprint, marker, candle, manila clasp envelopes, a different 60- to 100-piece puzzle for every sixteen people, construction paper (four sheets for each puzzle).

Before You Begin: Prepare gathering space and prayer space. Gather materials.

Mark the backs of the different puzzle pieces and the boxes with different symbols so that you can get the puzzles back into their boxes. Assemble one puzzle. Remove about twelve to fifteen center pieces and put them back in the box. Make sure the four sides to the puzzle are still intact. Divide the remaining puzzle into four equal parts, each with a corner. Break up one of the four parts and put the pieces into a manila envelope. Do the same with each other corner of that puzzle. Place a piece of one color of construction paper in each envelope and fasten the clasp. Do the same with the other puzzles, using a different color of paper for each puzzle.

On a sheet of newsprint write "Wis 7:7-8, 15-16."

Copy these Scripture citations on separate slips of paper: Gn 9:8-13; Gn 15:17-18; Gn 17:1-8; Ex 6:2-8; Ex 19:5-7; Dt 29:1; Ps 50:5; Is 42:6; Is 59:21; Jer 31:33; Mk 14:22-24; Lk 22:20; 2 Cor 3:4-6; Heb 7:20-22; Heb 9:18-20.

You will need one citation per family.

The Retreat

'Unraveling'

Ask families to get together in groups of eight to ten people. Have them stand in a close circle, extend both arms into the center and cross their forearms one over the other. Then have them grab two neighbors' hands, making sure they are not holding both hands of the same person. The object of the game is to become untangled without letting go of anyone's hand at any time. Give them about ten minutes or so to work it out. When they have untangled they will discover they are holding hands in a circle.

When the game is over ask them to sit down with family members and begin to process the game. How did they feel? What did they need to do to finally get unraveled? You hope they will point out the following three things: (1) They needed to stop once in a while and take stock of where they where and where they needed to go. (2) They needed to listen to each other. (3) They needed to work together.

Tell them this is good advice in any family situation. And today we are going to practice all three of the above: We are going to take some time out from our busy lives and take stock of who we are and whose we are by spending some time listening to each other and others and by working together.

'Family Stories'

Ask participants to sit together with their families. Distribute a copy of the Handout Page "Family Stories" and a pencil to each participant. Tell them they have five to ten minutes to fill out these handouts individually. Encourage them to fill in their answers by drawing a picture (even if it is only stick figures) in the appropriate boxes. (They may write out their answers if they prefer.) After they have all finished, they are to share their answers with one another.

After they are finished talking and listening to each other, see if they can come to a consensus on any of their answers. Finally, tell them to decide what they would like to share with the larger group about their family. They may choose any or all of what they came up with from their "Family Stories" page.

'Sharing Stories'

Gather all of the families in a large group. Ask each family to share who they are by giving their names, where they live, the ages of their children and how long they have been in the parish. Ask them to share one of the stories from the "Family Stories" handout.

Break

Take ten minutes to get refreshments, use the restrooms or just walk around a bit and mingle.

'Big Shoes/Little Shoes'

Ask youngsters to go to one side of the room and adults to the other. After they have gathered, tell them you have something you want them to do, but it must be done without any words. They will be forming two lines, one for children and another for adults. Ask them to line up according to shoe size, with the persons with the smallest feet at the front of each line and those with the largest at the ends.

Once they have finished lining up, put them into groups by asking the first and last persons in each line to form a group of four. You should end up with a fairly even intergenerational grouping. Ask this group to sit down and repeat the process until everyone is in a group. If you are left with three people at the end, they can form a group. If one or two are left, add each of them to another group.

'Puzzle-Solvers'

Give each group one of the manila envelopes with the following instructions: "Inside the envelopes are some puzzle pieces and a sheet of paper. Unfold the paper and use it as a mat on which to put your puzzle together. You have ten minutes to work together."

When the group have completed the puzzles, ask what they discovered. (They only had part of a puzzle.) Tell them to walk around to other groups and see if they can find other parts of their puzzle. If they do not discover it for themselves in a few minutes, let them know that the color of the mat is a clue. Finally, ask them to get together with the appropriate groups and put all their pieces together. When they begin to ask you about the missing pieces, tell them you will explain later.

'God Is a Puzzle'

Once they have finished their puzzles, ask them to gather closer. Begin by asking what they know about God. Listen to all their answers, encouraging both children and adults to speak. In your own words, tell them the following:

> "Everything you have said about God is true. There are probably many, many more things we can say. But even if all of the people in the whole world got together and shared everything they knew about God, our picture of God would still be like those puzzles you just put together. It would be incomplete.

"As long as we are on this earth, God will always remain a mystery, a puzzle we can spend our whole life trying to put together. One of the really important things to remember is that each of us has only a few of the pieces. We share our puzzle pieces by getting together with other folks and talking about our faith and how we see God. I can learn much about God from each of you, especially the youngsters. For some reason it seems that young people often have some of the most important pieces.

"Another place we can discover many other pieces to the puzzle of God is in this book. [Hold up Bible.] In here are all sorts of puzzle pieces. Some of them can be found in stories, some in poetry. Some of them can be found in prophecies and some in the history of a people, the Chosen People of God. And, of course, the biggest part of the puzzle can be found towards the back of this book—in the Gospels: the stories of Jesus, 'God With Us.'

"Do you remember when we sat around before the break and shared our family stories? We were getting to know each other. It works the same way if we want to get to know God better. We need to gather together and listen. Remember Jesus' promise: 'Wherever two or more are gathered, there I am.' Sharing our stories of faith and sharing the stories of Scripture is what our family program is all about. It offers you an opportunity to get to know God better in Scripture and by getting to know other families who are trying to do the same."

'Scripture Sharing'

Tell the participants that they are going to gather a few more pieces of the puzzle of God by looking at a few Scripture passages. Ask a member from each family to come pick up a Bible and a slip of paper with a Scripture citation. Tell them you are going to review how to break the "code" that tells them where to find their passage.

Begin by explaining that the Bible is not just one book. It is more like a library. It is a collection of books: history books, collections of proverbs, stories and poetry, a collection of letters (Epistles).

Invite them to thumb through the Bible and look at the names of the various books. Ask some of the children to read some of the names. Point out the page that shows how the names of the various books are abbreviated. Tell them to note where the Table of Contents is. These two pages will help them locate the book in the Bible.

Point to the name of the book in the Scripture citation on the newsprint. Ask them to find this book in their Bibles. Next point out the chapter number and ask them to find this also. Do the same with verses. When they have located the noted verses, ask someone to read them.

Ask them to look at their own Scripture citation and find the passage in their Bible. While they are locating their readings, you walk around to see if anyone needs help. When they are finished, ask them to choose a family member to read the verse during the Closing Prayer. Tell them to use their citation slips as bookmarks for their passages and to bring their Bibles with them as they gather for prayer.

Closing Prayer

Light the candle and, if you feel the group would be comfortable, begin with a song. Say the following prayer, or make up your own opening prayer:

"Lord, we praise you and we thank you for the gift of life, especially for sharing the gift of your own life with us. Help us to grow closer to you, to people in our own family and to all those gathered here with us. Help us to put the pieces together as we come to know you better. Help us to be aware of your presence in our lives and to share that awareness with one another. Help us to listen to one another and to your words in Scripture. Amen."

Ask someone from each family to read the group's passage, first telling the participants to listen carefully to see what the passages have in common. When they are finished reading, ask if anyone can tell you what was the same in each passage. (They all had to do with covenant.)

Explain what a covenant is by using your own words or the following:

"The word *covenant* in the secular world of biblical times referred to a contract or agreement between two people or between tribes of people. In Scripture the word is used to describe the relationship God has with all people. As we just heard, there are all sorts of covenants in the Bible. One important covenant, however, is the one God first made with Abraham and continues to make with us. That covenant is very simple: God's love will always be faithful. All God asks of us is to return that love.

"You are invited to take part in another covenant. This covenant is between the individuals gathered here (as well as the other people who are a part of our parish 'Family Faith' group). It is a pledge that says you will do your best to be open to God's call to grow closer to God by scheduling some time with your own family as well as with members of our larger parish family. If you decide that you as a family will not be able to be a part of our parish's 'Family Faith' group, please let me know. If you decide to say yes to this invitation, please come to our next gathering, where we will solemnize our covenant."

Read or have someone else read Ephesians 3:14-21. End with the Our Father.

Family Stories

Saddest thing:

Happiest thing:

This is what I most like to do with my family:

Scariest thing:

Our best family vacation:

Advent Retreat

Advent is a time for waiting, for preparing for the coming of the Lord. This two-and-a-half-hour retreat gathers families to wait and prepare together. The icebreaker, "Christmas Bingo," is an informal way to get people, young and old, to mingle and meet in a comfortable setting. The activity, "Family Gifts," asks them to imagine the perfect gift for each member of their family—a fun way to give parents and children some insight into other family members' wants, needs and dreams.

Families will also take some time to talk to each other about how they celebrate Christmas in their homes. Perhaps the opportunity to hear about other families' Christmas traditions will enrich their own Christmas.

Finally, the gathered families will spend the majority of the time decorating a Jesse Tree together. The main focus of this activity is to learn a little more about the people who came before Jesus, who prepared for Jesus' coming hundreds, even thousands, of years before he was born. They were Jesus' ancestors and our own ancestors in faith.

Schedule (155 minutes):
- "Christmas Bingo"
  (large group, 15 minutes)
- "Family Gifts"
  (family groups, 20 minutes)
- "Christmas Stories"
  (large group, 30 minutes)
- Break (10 minutes)
- Explanation of the Jesse Tree Tradition
  (large group, 10 minutes)
- Creating ornaments for the Jesse Tree
  (family groups, 30 minutes)
- "Ornament Stories"
  (large group, 25 minutes)
- Closing Prayer
  (large group, 15 minutes)

Materials Needed: Bibles; pencils; a copy of "Christmas Bingo" and "Family Gifts" (pages 103 and 105) for each person; a copy of "The Jesse Tree" (pages 107 to 117) for each family; ornament hooks; string, scissors and tacky glue; an artificial Christmas tree or a tree branch; suggested materials for ornaments (felt, fabric, yarn, glitter, pipe cleaners, cardboard, empty tuna cans, margarine bowls with lids, lids to other containers, cotton balls, fringe, craft sticks, pieces of balsa wood, paper plates, buttons, beads, bottle tops, construction paper).

Before You Begin: It would be great if the Jesse Tree could be part of the parish's Advent environment. Check with the pastor or staff to see if the tree can be placed in the gathering space or some other appropriate spot where the whole parish can see it.

Set the Environment: Gather supplies and make copies of the Handout Page "Christmas Bingo" (page 103).

The Retreat

'Christmas Bingo'

Distribute pencils and copies of the "Christmas Bingo" Handout Page to all. Ask adults to help any child who is too young to read. Give the following directions for the icebreaker: "The object of this game is to collect as many names as possible in the appropriate squares of the sheet. A person can sign only one square. You have seven minutes to meet and greet as many people as possible."

'Family Gifts'

Pass out the Handout Page "Family Gifts." Explain that participants are to think of a perfect gift for each member of their family. Money is no object, and the gift need not be something one can buy in a store. Ask people to take some time thinking about each family member before they decide. Tell them this is a quiet activity; the gifts are to be a surprise. They can either write or draw their gifts in the appropriate spaces on the Handout Page. Make sure they mark whom each gift is for. If they need more space, they may use the other side of the paper. They will have about five to ten minutes to complete their papers.

After about ten minutes (more time if needed) ask them to gather in family groups. Remind them not to share their "gifts" until you tell them. When everyone is ready, inform them they will have ten minutes to talk about two things: (1) They are to share the gifts they chose for each other. (2) They are to talk about Christmas. How do they celebrate Christmas at their house? Do they have any special traditions or any special Christmas memories? Let them know they will be asked to talk about their family Christmas in the large group.

'Christmas Stories'

After fifteen minutes or so, ask families to gather as a large group. Allow about thirty minutes (more or less as needed) for them to tell how they celebrate Christmas at their house.

Break

Take ten minutes to get refreshments, use the restrooms or just walk around a bit and mingle.

Explanation of the Jesse Tree Tradition

Say in your own words:

> "We are going to decorate a very special tree. We are going to make ornaments for a Jesse Tree. This Advent activity is like a family tree, a way for us to remember Jesus' ancestors. We will talk about people who lived long before Jesus was born and some people who were born only a short time before him. The ornaments we make will be reminders of these men and women. They are important not only to Jesus but also to us, because they are our ancestors, too. They are the mothers and fathers of our faith.
>
> "The tree is named after a man called Jesse, who lived a thousand years before Jesus. He was Jesus' many-greats-grandfather. This is what the prophet Isaiah had to say about Jesse: 'A shoot shall come out from the stump of Jesse,/and a branch shall grow out of his roots' [Isaiah 11:1]. Later Isaiah tells us that the Holy One will come from Jesse and his family. He will be a person of peace and justice. He will be wise and understanding and strong—strong enough to defeat all that is evil. We will learn more about Jesse when we hear about Jesus' other relatives. But first we will make ornaments to hang on our Jesse Tree.

"I have gathered all sorts of materials for you to work with. Each family will receive the name of one of Jesus' ancestors. After you read about the person, try to decide on a symbol that could represent them. If you have trouble figuring something out, the words in bold print will give you an idea of some traditional symbols. Be as creative as you like. If possible, try to make your ornament three-dimensional. Do not forget to put a string on it so that we can hang it on our tree later."

Point out where the supplies are located and tell them they will have about thirty minutes to read about the person and make an ornament.

Allow enough time for families to work together. Walk around to all the groups to make sure they understood your instructions and to see if they need any additional supplies.

'Ornament Stories'

Ask each family to stand when you call their Jesse Tree figure's name. Ask them to read what they read about their person; encourage them to add anything else they may know. Ask them to hold up their ornament and explain how it represents the person whose name they chose. If more than one family has the same name, ask them to take turns responding. Make sure they both explain their ornaments. Continue until everyone has had a chance.

Here are the names that are to make up your Jesse Tree: Adam and Eve, Abraham and Sarah, Noah, Jacob, Joseph, Moses, Ruth, Jesse, David, Solomon, Isaiah and Micah, Jonah, Joseph, Mary.

Closing Prayer

Ask people to gather around the tree. Make sure each group has a hook with which to hang its ornament. Tell them you will start with a song, then a reading from the Gospel of John and a litany of Jesus' ancestors. Every time they hear the words, "and we wait, too," in the litany, they respond, "Come, Lord Jesus, come!" When they hear the name of their person they are to hang their ornament on the tree. (You might want to stand next to the folks who have Adam and Eve so that you can give them a nudge if they need one.) Finally, let them know that you will conclude the service by saying together the prayer Jesus gave us, the Our Father.

Opening Song: "O Come, O Come Emmanuel" or any other appropriate Advent song.

Reading: John 1:1-5.

Jesse Tree Litany

"God's own breath gave life to our first ancestors, and God's own breath fills us. We were loved into being, just as they were. We are called and chosen, just as they were. For thousands of years there has been a people who have been in covenant with God, and now we are those people. It is our covenant. We trust God to be with us always, and we promise God to be faithful. We wait, as our ancestors in faith waited, for the coming of the Lord. Together let us remember all of those people who went before us, witnessing to the one true God—a people who knew how to wait."

Respond, "Come, Lord Jesus," after each sentence.

"Adam and Eve waited outside the gates of Paradise, and we wait, too. Come, Lord Jesus.

"Noah waited and waited for the rains to stop, and we wait, too.

"Abraham and Sarah waited and waited for their promised baby, and we wait, too.

"Jacob waited seven long years for his promised bride, and we wait, too.

"Joseph waited and waited in a country far from home, and we wait, too.

"Moses waited for forty years in the desert, and we wait, too.

"Ruth waited faithfully at the side of her mother-in-law, and we wait, too.

"Jesse waited for one of his sons to be chosen, and we wait, too.

"David waited for just the right time to fling the stone, and we wait, too.

"Solomon waited and waited for the temple to be built, and we wait, too.

"Isaiah and Micah waited and waited for people to listen, and we wait, too.

"Jonah waited three days in the belly of a whale, and we wait, too.

"Joseph waited to find a comfortable place for Mary, and we wait, too.

"Mary waited nine long months for the birth of her baby, and we wait, too."

Closing Prayer: The Our Father

Christmas Bingo

Try to fill in as many of the squares below as you can with people's names. A person can only sign or initial one box. People can only sign squares that are true for them.

I have gotten a tie for Christmas.	I have gone caroling.	I know who Jesus' foster father is.	I have stuffed a turkey.	I have hung up my stocking.
I know what town Jesus was born in.	I have been in a Christmas play.	I like eggnog.	I have traveled over five hundred miles for Christmas.	I can name three of Santa's reindeer.
I can sing "Jingle Bells."	I know where Jesus was laid when he was born.	FREE SPACE	I have sat on Santa's lap.	I have a real tree for Christmas.
I can laugh like Santa.	I make cookies.	I know how many Wise Men came.	I go to midnight Mass.	I know what I want for Christmas.
I keep my tree up until Epiphany.	I have started Christmas shopping.	I have a tree-top angel.	I like candy canes.	I know Jesus' mother's name.

Family Gifts

In the gift boxes below draw or write down what you think would be the perfect present for each member of your family. If you need more gift boxes, draw them on the other side of this page. Be sure to put the person's name on the tag.

Before you begin, take some time to think about the people in your family. If they could have anything they want and money is no problem, what do you think they would like to receive from you?

The Jesse Tree

Reproduce the materials below and cut the paragraphs apart to hand out as references. Let people know that the words in bold type are the traditional symbols for a person. They may choose this symbol or decide on one of their own.

ADAM AND EVE are the names given to the first man and woman. This is how they came to be: God created the whole universe. God made the sun and moon, the earth and everything on it—all the plants and flowers, all the animals and birds and fish. God also created people. People were God's special creation because God's own breath gave them life. Adam and Eve were very happy living in the paradise God had created. They were very happy, that is, until they made a big mistake. They disobeyed God. They ate the **fruit** from the one and only tree that God had specifically asked them to avoid. When Adam and Eve chose to disobey God, they could no longer live in paradise. They had to leave. Now they had to work hard. Now they would get sick. Life was much more difficult because they chose not to listen to God.

ABRAHAM AND SARAH lived in a time when people worshiped many gods. But Abraham and Sarah chose to worship only the one true God. They left their home and traveled thousands of miles because God asked them to do so. They rode on **camels** and they lived in **tents** all their lives. God promised Abraham and Sarah that they would have many, many descendants. (A descendant is a child or grandchild or great-great-great-grandchild.) God made a special covenant with Abraham and Sarah: "I will always take care of you and be faithful to you. And you must always believe and be faithful only to me, the one true God." Abraham and Sarah had no children. The one thing they wanted most of all was a child of their own, but they were very old. They did not know how they could possibly have any descendants since they did not have even one child. They forgot that nothing is impossible for God. Sure enough, God was true to the covenant. God took care of them. Even though Sarah was very, very old, she gave birth to a son. They named him Isaac. God kept the covenant. God took good care of Abraham and Sarah.

NOAH was a very special man. He lived a good life when everyone around him was very wicked. This is the story of Noah and the **ark** that he built, the story of a great flood. The flood happened because wherever God looked on the earth wicked people were doing evil things. God decided to start over. God told Noah to build a huge ark, a boat large enough to carry his whole family plus two of every animal on earth. Noah followed God's instructions. He built the ark and gathered the animals and his family on board. Then it started to rain. It rained for forty days straight. For one hundred and fifty days the water got higher and higher. Finally, Noah noticed that the water was starting to go down. Noah waited another forty days and then he sent out a bird to find out if there was dry land around. The bird flew away but came back in a little while. There was no land nearby. Noah sent out a second bird, a dove. This time the bird came back with an olive branch in its beak. The olive branch meant that they were close to dry land. They were saved. God made another covenant with Noah. God promised that the earth would never be destroyed again by a great flood. God put a rainbow in the sky. The **rainbow** was a sign of the covenant between God and all living creatures.

JACOB was the son of Isaac and Rebekah, grandson to Abraham and Sarah. His father wanted him to marry a woman from among his kinspeople. On Jacob's way to their land he had a dream. He saw a **ladder** going up into the heavens and messengers going up and down on it. In the dream, he also saw God standing next to him. God made a covenant with Jacob—the same covenant that God had made with Jacob's grandfather, Abraham. God said, "I will give you many children. They will have a land of their own." When Jacob got to the place of his kinspeople, he stopped for a drink of water. At the well he met Rachel, a woman of his father's family. This, he decided, was the woman he wanted to marry. Rachel's father told him that if he worked for seven years he could marry his beautiful daughter. Jacob agreed, but after the seven years Jacob was tricked into marrying another daughter, Leah. Jacob still wanted to marry Rachel, but he had to agree to work another seven years for his father-in-law. Now Jacob had two wives. (In those days men were allowed to have more than one wife.) Leah and Rachel gave Jacob twelve sons. Jacob's two favorite sons were Joseph and Benjamin, the two sons of Rachel.

JOSEPH was Jacob's favorite son. His father loved him so much that he gave him a special **coat of many colors**. Joseph's brothers were jealous of him. They sold Joseph to some passing merchants and told their father that the boy had been killed by a wild animal. Joseph ended up in Egypt. When he was able to help the pharaoh (the king), the pharaoh freed Joseph. Joseph convinced the pharaoh to store up enough food to feed the whole country for seven years. The pharaoh made him a very powerful leader. Now Joseph was no longer a slave. When a great famine fell on the land, Joseph was the one who gave out food. The famine was so great that all the countries around Egypt also ran out of food. When Joseph's own family became hungry, Jacob sent his older sons to Egypt to buy food so they would not starve. When they went to Joseph to ask for food, Joseph's brothers did not recognize him at first, but Joseph knew them. Instead of punishing his brothers for selling him to the merchants, Joseph forgave them. Joseph brought his whole family to Egypt. There they could live and not be afraid of starving.

MOSES was born in Egypt many, many years after Joseph died. At that time the Hebrew people were slaves. When he was a baby, Moses was adopted by the new pharaoh's daughter. The people in the palace did not know that Moses was a Jew. When Moses grew up he saw how his people were being mistreated. When he saw a soldier beating one of the Jews, he killed the soldier. Moses had to run away and hide. One day, when he was up in the hills, Moses saw something very strange. He saw **a burning bush**. The bush kept burning and burning, but it never burned up. When he went up to the bush, Moses heard God's voice. God told Moses to go back to Egypt and to help the Hebrew people become free. Moses was supposed to lead the people to the Promised Land. God convinced Moses that he would be able to do it because God's power would be with him. After Egypt suffered many plagues, the pharaoh finally let the Hebrew people go. Moses led them into the desert, where they walked for forty years. They had many adventures. During that time, Moses received the Ten Commandments from God. Finally, they reached the Promised Land, but Moses died before the people entered it.

RUTH was a Moabite woman. She was not a Jew, but she married a man who was from Bethlehem. When her husband died she returned to the Promised Land with her mother-in-law, Naomi. When they got to Bethlehem, they were very poor. Ruth had to go out to the fields and follow the harvesters as they cut the **sheaves of wheat**. She collected the grain that the workers had left behind. This is how she and Naomi were able to eat. The owner of the field, Boaz, was a distant cousin of Ruth's husband. He told the workers to be kind to Ruth and make sure no one hurt her. One day Naomi told Ruth to go to where Boaz was sleeping and lie down at his feet. Naomi said if she slept there all night, then Boaz would marry her. And that is what happened. Boaz married Ruth and they were both very happy. They had a son whose name was Obed. Obed was Jesse's father. So Ruth was Jesse's grandmother.

JESSE was a descendant of Ruth and Boaz. He lived in Bethlehem and had seven sons. One day a holy man came to visit the town. He was looking for the next king of Israel. God had sent him to Bethlehem to anoint the chosen one. When the holy man got to the town, God told him that the next king would be one of Jesse's sons. Jesse introduced his oldest son to the man. "Surely, this must be the next king," thought the man. "He is so handsome, so big and so strong." But God told the man he was wrong, to keep looking. Jesse introduced all his other sons to the holy man, but none of them was the chosen one, either. Finally, when the man asked Jesse if he had any other sons, Jesse told him that his youngest son, still a boy, was in the fields watching the sheep. The man asked Jesse to send for him. The young boy was David. He was not very big; he was not very strong, but he was the chosen one. The holy man anointed him right there and then. Another prophet, Isaiah, called the Messiah who was to come the sprout or **branch** of Jesse because God told him that the Messiah would be a descendant of David.

DAVID was the greatest king Israel ever had. He grew up a shepherd. He was also a very fine musician. David played a small **harp**. When he was still very young he killed a giant enemy soldier named Goliath. The giant laughed when David stood in front of him and told him he would win the fight because God was on his side. David killed Goliath with a stone from his slingshot. He saved his whole country. The man who was king became frightened because he could see how popular David was with the people. For many years David had to keep running and hiding just to stay alive. Some people say that this was when David wrote many of the psalms that are in our Bible. Eventually David was crowned king. He was a very wise and brave king. He made Israel a strong nation, a nation that was respected everywhere. The people all loved David.

SOLOMON was David's son. He became the king when David died, almost a thousand years before Jesus was born. Solomon was responsible for building much of Jerusalem. He built the great **Temple** in the capital city so that the people would have a central place to gather and worship God. One day Solomon had a dream. In the dream God told the young king that anything he asked for would be his. After Solomon thought for a while, he asked God to give him an understanding heart and the wisdom to be a good king. God was very pleased with Solomon. God told him that because he had not asked for riches or long life but for the wisdom to be a good ruler, he would receive all three. Solomon became very rich. He was also considered a very wise person. He is traditionally considered the father of Israelite wisdom and wisdom literature. The years Solomon was king were peaceful and prosperous for the Hebrew people.

ISAIAH and **MICAH** were great prophets. (Prophets were people who warned the Hebrews not to worship other gods but to be faithful to the one true God, Yahweh. They kept reminding the people about their covenant with Yahweh.) Micah told the people that Yahweh wanted them to do just three things: to act justly, to love tenderly and to walk humbly with their God. He also told the people that the greatest ruler of the world would come from Bethlehem. Isaiah was one of the greatest prophets. He lived about seven hundred years before Jesus was born. Isaiah lived during a time when many of the Hebrew people had been captured by their enemies and were forced to move out of Israel. Isaiah offered the people hope. He told them to stay faithful to Yahweh. He told them that Yahweh would send them a Messiah. Prophets are often symbolized by a **rose**.

JONAH was another prophet. He lived about five hundred years before Jesus was born. God told Jonah to go to a certain city and tell them to repent and turn to God. Jonah did not want to go there because the people in the city were the enemies of the Hebrew people. There is a wonderful story about how God convinced Jonah to go to the city: After Jonah refused to go where God wanted to send him, he found himself tossed overboard from the ship he was sailing in. Suddenly a huge **whale** came along and swallowed Jonah. Jonah lived in the belly of the whale for three days before the whale spit him out onto the shore. Jonah learned the hard way that Yahweh wanted all people, not just the Hebrews, to believe in one true God.

JOSEPH was the man chosen by God to help Mary raise Jesus. He was Jesus' foster father. He worked as a carpenter in a town called Nazareth. He used hammers and planes and other **tools** to build tables and chairs and other furniture for people. One night Joseph had a dream. In the dream an angel told Joseph to marry Mary. And that is what he did. Joseph was a descendant of David, so when it was time to go and sign up for the census, he took his wife, Mary, to Bethlehem, David's city. That is where Jesus was born. Joseph was a very kind and gentle person. He took good care of Mary and Jesus.

MARY was Jesus' mother. She was especially chosen by God, but she still had to say yes. One day when Mary was alone, an angel came to her and told her she was going to be the mother of a son. The baby would be called the Son of the Most High. Mary told the angel that it was impossible for her to have a child because she was a virgin. The angel told her to trust in God, that the Holy Spirit would take care of everything. The angel said that all things were possible because God was all-powerful. Mary said yes and became the mother of Jesus. Mary took good care of Jesus when he was a little baby and all through his growing-up years. She fed him and washed his clothes. She bandaged his cuts and kissed his bruises. Before Jesus died he asked his special friend to take care of Mary. Then he asked Mary to take care of his special friend. Since Jesus is our brother, Mary is also our mother. Her symbol is a **lily**.

Jesus Retreat

During this two-and-a-half-hour retreat, families will learn more about Jesus as well as about each other. The opening icebreaker pairs young and older people by asking them to put together some of the many names we have given to Jesus throughout the years. The pairs stay together, sometimes joining with another pair, to read a Scripture passage and come up with their own creative way to retell their reading to the larger group. Once everyone has regathered, they listen to each other as they proclaim the Good News though storyboards, skits, advertisements, stories and, finally, a free-hanging mobile that is used as a prop to retell the passion, death and resurrection of Jesus.

During "Family Time," families are given time to talk about their favorite stories of Jesus. As they discuss the qualities that made Jesus such an extraordinary person, they are also asked to look inside themselves to discover which of those qualities they most need.

In the Closing Prayer, we remember Jesus by all the names we identified in our opening activity and end with family members blessing each other and praying together for the gifts they need to live their lives as faithfully to God and others as Jesus did.

Schedule (145 minutes):
• "Names of Jesus"
    (15 minutes)
• Explanation of "Sharing the Good News"
    (large group, 15 minutes)
• "Sharing the Good News" Project
    (pairs, 30 minutes)
• Break (10 minutes)
• "Sharing the Good News"
    (large group, 45 minutes)
• "Favorite Jesus Stories"
    (15 minutes)
• Closing Prayer
    (family groups, 15 minutes)

Materials needed: newsprint, pencils, crayons, markers, paper plates, string, glue sticks, scissors, Bibles, slips of paper, copies of "Names of Jesus" (page 123) and "Life Events," "Parables," "Miracles" and "Teachings" notes (pages 125 to 139).

Before You Begin: Prepare prayer space. Make copies of Handout Pages (pages 123 to 139). Cut apart the names of Jesus and the "Sharing the Good News" notes. Gather supplies.

Write on a piece of newsprint: "What is your favorite part of Jesus' story?" Write on another: "Name someone you know or have read about who reminds you of Jesus. Tell why." Hang newsprint that says, "Names of Jesus." Have glue sticks nearby.

The Retreat

'Names of Jesus'

Once people are gathered and you know how many will be participating, cut the appropriate number of names of Jesus (one for every two people). Put the left halves in one envelope for the children and the right halves in another envelope for the adults.

The object of this game is for each person to find the other half of their slip of paper. When the two halves are together they will spell out a word or phrase. Make sure each person receives a half-paper from the right age-group envelope. When you are ready, ask everyone to find the other half, and with the newfound partner glue the word or phrase onto the newsprint on the wall. When they are finished, partners are to sit together.

While people are involved in the icebreaker, decide on how many Scripture notes you will need. Use all the "Life Events" and "Jesus' Last Days." (If you have fewer than sixteen people, decide which life event to eliminate.) Additional notes may be taken in equal proportion from the remaining categories.

'Sharing the Good News' Project

Ask the children to read the words and phrases that have been glued to the newsprint. Ask them if they know to whom all the words refer.

In your own words tell them the following:

> "Today we are going to be talking about Jesus. We are going to learn more about the events in Jesus' life, about his teachings and about his last days. We will hear about Jesus' miracles and about the stories he told. Today all of you are going to be the teachers. You will be working in pairs or groups of four to tell the Good News of Jesus Christ to each other."

(The number in each group and the number of groups will depend on how many are present.)

Explain the categories (see below). [Groups may choose a category or you may just give each a Good News Note to work with.] Pass out the notes, which explain what to do and contain the Scripture reference. Hand out Bibles. Ask participants to read their cards. (If necessary, review how to find Scripture citations in the Bible.) Let participants know where they will find the supplies and ask if there are any questions. Tell them they will have thirty minutes to read their Scripture passages and complete their projects.

Walk around while participants are working to answer questions or offer help. Check each group or pair to make sure they understand the directions on the note cards.

Categories

Life Events: After reading the Scripture passage together, participants will draw a storyboard of the event—something like a comic strip version. Later they will retell the story with illustrations in the large group. One pair of participants or more for each event.

Stories: After reading Jesus' story from Scripture, participants will write their own modern-day story that has the same message. Assign one pair of participants or more for each story.

Miracles: After reading the miracle story, this group will act out the story when the large group regathers. Assign two pairs (a group of four) for each miracle story.

Teachings: After reading the Scripture passage that gives the basic teaching of Jesus, participants will come up with their own ad that "sells" this message to the public. Assign one pair or more for each Scripture passage.

Jesus' Last Days: After reading the Scripture passage about the last days of Jesus' life, this group will make a mobile with at least five symbols that say something about what happened during those last days. They will retell the story as they share their mobile with the large group. Assign two pairs (a group of four).

Break

Take ten minutes to get refreshments, use the restrooms or just walk around a bit and mingle.

'Sharing the Good News'

Gather participants into the large group. Ask them to note the number written on their card. Tell them that this is roughly the order of their turns to present. Explain that some numbers will be skipped because not all of the Scripture notes were used. Ask them to listen as you call the numbers.

You may begin by saying, "The gospel, the Good News according to the families of (*your parish's name*)." Call numbers in sequence until all have had a chance to share their part of the Jesus story.

'Favorite Jesus Stories'

Ask family members to sit together. Put up newsprint that has the following two questions written on it: (1) "What is your favorite part of the story about Jesus? (It need not be one of the stories that was presented today.)" (2) "Name someone you know or have read about who reminds you of Jesus. Tell why." Ask them to take a couple of minutes to think about their answers. Tell them they will have ten minutes to talk to each other about their answers.

After ten minutes, put up a sheet of clean newsprint and ask families to help you list all the different good qualities they can think of (strong, patient and so on) that describe Jesus. When you have completed the list, ask them to write down one of Jesus' qualities they wish they

had more of. Tell them they will be sharing what they wrote down with the rest of their family during the Closing Prayer. Hand out slips of paper and pencils. When families are finished, ask them to gather for prayer.

Closing Prayer

Before beginning, make sure each family member has the slip of paper from the last activity. If the group is not sure how to bless each other, you might model this for them. Bless a volunteer on the forehead, using your thumb to make a small cross and saying, "I bless you in the name of the Father, and of the Son, and of the Holy Spirit. Amen."

Gather in a circle around a table that has a candle and a Bible on it. Put the newsprint with all of Jesus' names on it in front of the table. Say the following prayer,

> "Jesus, you are (*say all the names on the newsprint, leaving "brother" and "friend" for last*). Help us to remember that you will always be with us."

Read John 15:15-17 or another appropriate reading. Tell families that you are going to ask them to bless each other now. Adults will bless children, children will bless adults. First, however, they are to give the person who is blessing them their slip of paper. The person who is doing the blessing is asked to read what is written on the paper and say the following while making the Sign of the Cross:

> "May you be blessed with Jesus' _____ (*fill in the quality written on the slip of paper*). In the name of the Father, and of the Son, and of the Holy Spirit. Amen."

End with the Our Father or a closing song.

Names of Jesus

Lamb of God	Nazarene	King of Glory
Prince of Peace	The Truth	Savior
Mary's Son	The Light	The Word
Son of God	Messiah	The Way
Teacher	Brother	Good Shepherd
The Christ	Friend	Miracle-Worker

Life Events

1) Jesus' Birth (Luke 2:1-20)

After you have read the Scripture passage together, take a sheet of newsprint and fold it in four. Open up the newsprint and draw in the rectangles pictures that tell the story of what you just read. (Stick figures are fine.) Make sure you tell the story in order.

2) Jesus' Baptism (Matthew 3:1-6, 13-17)

After you have read the Scripture passage together, take a sheet of newsprint and fold it in four. Open up the newsprint and draw in the rectangles pictures that tell the story of what you just read. (Stick figures are fine.) Make sure you tell the story in order.

3) The Temptation in the Desert (Matthew 4:1-11)

After you have read the Scripture passage together, take a sheet of newsprint and fold it in four. Open up the newsprint and draw in the rectangles pictures that tell the story of what you just read. (Stick figures are fine.) Make sure you tell the story in order.

9) Jesus Calls the First Disciples (Luke 5:1-11)

After you have read the Scripture passage together, take a sheet of newsprint and fold it in four. Open up the newsprint and draw in the rectangles pictures that tell the story of what you just read. (Stick figures are fine.) Make sure you tell the story in order.

14) The Transfiguration (Mark 9:2-8)

After you have read the Scripture passage together, take a sheet of newsprint and fold it in four. Open up the newsprint and draw in the rectangles pictures that tell the story of what you just read. (Stick figures are fine.) Make sure you tell the story in order.

19) Blessing the Children (Mark 10:13-16)

After you have read the Scripture passage together, take a sheet of newsprint and fold it in four. Open up the newsprint and draw in the rectangles pictures that tell the story of what you just read. (Stick figures are fine.) Make sure you tell the story in order.

Parables

6) The Story of the Sower (Matthew 13:1-9, 18-23)

Jesus liked to teach people by telling stories. These stories were called parables. After you have read Jesus' story, talk about what you think the message is. Write your own modern-day story that has the same message.

---

10) The Story of the Good Samaritan (Luke 10:25-37)

Jesus liked to teach people by telling stories. These stories were called parables. After you have read Jesus' story, talk about what you think the message is. Write your own modern-day story that has the same message.

---

13) The Story of the Lost Sheep (Matthew 18:12-14)

Jesus liked to teach people by telling stories. These stories were called parables. After you have read Jesus' story, talk about what you think the message is. Write your own modern-day story that has the same message.

---

17) The Story of the Prodigal Son (Luke 15:11-32)

Jesus liked to teach people by telling stories. These stories were called parables. After you have read Jesus' story, talk about what you think the message is. Write your own modern-day story that has the same message.

20) The Story of the Workers in the Vineyard (Matthew 20:1-16)

Jesus liked to teach people by telling stories. These stories were called parables. After you have read Jesus' story, talk about what you think the message is. Write your own modern-day story that has the same message.

23) The Story of the Talents (Matthew 25:14-30)

Jesus liked to teach people by telling stories. These stories were called parables. After you have read Jesus' story, talk about what you think the message is. Write your own modern-day story that has the same message.

Additional Scripture Passages
The Rich Fool (Luke 13:16-21)
The Great Feast (Luke 14:15-24)
The Unjust Servant (Luke 16:1-13)
The Wicked Tenants (Mark 12:1-11)
The Ten Bridesmaids (Matthew 25:1-13)

Miracles

4) The Wedding Feast of Cana (John 2:1-11)

Jesus helped many people by the miracles he worked. After you have read together the miracle story noted above, decide who will play the different roles. Practice acting out the story.

7) The Calming of the Storm (Mark 4:35-41)

Jesus helped many people by the miracles he worked. After you have read together the miracle story noted above, decide who will play the different roles. Practice acting out the story.

11) The Cure of the Centurion's Servant (Matthew 8:5-13)

Jesus helped many people by the miracles he worked. After you have read together the miracle story noted above, decide who will play the different roles. Practice acting out the story.

16) The Miracles of the Loaves and Fishes (Luke 9:10-17)

Jesus helped many people by the miracles he worked. After you have read together the miracle story noted above, decide who will play the different roles. Practice acting out the story.

21) The Healing of the Blind Man (Mark 8:22-26)

Jesus helped many people by the miracles he worked. After you have read together the miracle story noted above, decide who will play the different roles. Practice acting out the story.

24) The Cure of Jairus's Daughter (Mark 5:21-43)

Jesus helped many people by the miracles he worked. After you have read together the miracle story noted above, decide who will play the different roles. Practice acting out the story.

Additional Scripture Passages
Cure of the Paralytic (Luke 5:17-26)
Jesus Walks on Water (Mark 6:45-52)
Cure of the Blind Man (Mark 10:46-52)
Cure of the Epileptic Boy (Matthew 17:14-20)
The Raising of Lazarus (John 11:1-44)

Teachings

5) The Beatitudes (Matthew 5:1-12)

Read the Scripture passage that gives the basic teaching of Jesus. Pretend that you are an advertising executive who wants to get this message out to the public. Draw an ad that could be used in a magazine, newspaper or on TV. Work out the details on regular paper before you put it on a large sheet of newsprint.

8) The Salt of the Earth (Matthew 5:13-16)

Read the Scripture passage that gives the basic teaching of Jesus. Pretend that you are an advertising executive who wants to get this message out to the public. Draw an ad that could be used in a magazine, newspaper or on TV. Work out the details on regular paper before you put it on a large sheet of newsprint.

12) God and Money (Matthew 6:24)

Read the Scripture passage that gives the basic teaching of Jesus. Pretend that you are an advertising executive who wants to get this message out to the public. Draw an ad that could be used in a magazine, newspaper or on TV. Work out the details on regular paper before you put it on a large sheet of newsprint.

5) Trust in God (Matthew 6:25-34)

Read the Scripture passage that gives the basic teaching of Jesus. Pretend that you are an advertising executive who wants to get this message out to the public. Draw an ad that could be used in a magazine, newspaper or on TV. Work out the details on regular paper before you put it on a large sheet of newsprint.

18) God Revealed to Simple People (Matthew 11:25-27)

Read the Scripture passage that gives the basic teaching of Jesus. Pretend that you are an advertising executive who wants to get this message out to the public. Draw an ad that could be used in a magazine, newspaper or on TV. Work out the details on regular paper before you put it on a large sheet of newsprint.

22) Forgiving Injuries (Matthew 18:21-22)

Read the Scripture passage that gives the basic teaching of Jesus. Pretend that you are an advertising executive who wants to get this message out to the public. Draw an ad that could be used in a magazine, newspaper or on TV. Work out the details on regular paper before you put it on a large sheet of newsprint.

25) Jesus' Last Days (Mark 11:1-10; 14:12—16:8)

Read together the Scripture passages about the last days of Jesus' life. Decide on at least five symbols that say something about what happened on those days. Draw, color and cut out the symbols. To make a mobile, attach the symbols to the paper plate with string. Be ready to retell the story of those last days as you share your mobile with the group.

Signs, Symbols and Sacraments Retreat

In this retreat participants learn and pray about all the things mentioned in the title. Rather than one closing ritual, this retreat includes three rituals, each focused on a symbol of sacramental initiation: water, oil or bread. The activities in this retreat are designed to help people understand better what sacraments are about.

The first activity asks the participants to imagine what the world would be like if we all lived according to the plan of God. After sharing these ideas on newsprint, participants talk about what the world is like today. These activities lead into a discussion of the mission of Jesus and the mission of the Church. After a brief explanation of sacrament, participants gather in groups of five or six to read several scriptural references and put together a collage that represents a symbol of initiation. Following a discussion of the symbols, the day ends with the last ritual, which gives everyone an opportunity to share bread and personal greetings.

Schedule (90 minutes):
- Water Ritual
    (large group, 10 minutes)
- "The World According to God"
    (family groups, 20 minutes)
- "Sharing Our Worlds"
    (large group, 10 minutes)
- "A Sacrament for the Real World"
    (large group, 10 minutes)
- Break (10 minutes)
- Oil Ritual
    (family groups, 10 minutes)
- "Signs and Symbols"
    (intergenerational groups, 10 minutes)
- Bread Ritual
    (large group, 10 minutes)

Materials Needed: Bibles, magazines, scissors, glue, markers, tape, oil, tablecloth, clear glass cruet or small cream pitcher, water, glass pitcher, large glass bowl, large loaf of unsliced bread, platter or basket, candle, newsprint, paper cups, poster board.

Before You Begin: Prepare prayer space with a table in the center. Place on top of the table the cloth, candle, Bible, bowl, pitcher filled with water.

Draw large circles that take up almost all the space on newsprint. You will need one sheet of newsprint per four or five people, plus one for you.

Cut one of the poster boards the long way, leaving you with a piece at least nine by twenty-seven inches.

Write the definition of *sacrament* on newsprint. (See italicized sentence ending at the top of page 144.)

Prepare three sheets of newsprint for "Signs and Symbols."

Gather materials. Cut the sides of the paper cups down to about two inches to make small bowls.

The Retreat

Water Ritual

Gather everyone in a circle around a table on which there is a candle, a large bowl and a pitcher of water. Have someone ready to pour the water from the pitcher into the bowl when it is time. Make sure they understand they are to hold the pitcher several inches above the bowl and pour the water slowly while the blessing is being said.

Begin by explaining that we are getting closer and closer to the great feast of Easter. Today we will be talking about signs, symbols and sacraments. Therefore, rather than just celebrating one prayer ritual, we will gather three times to pray together.

Ask participants to stand and extend their hand toward the water as the water is blessed. As the following blessing is said, the water is poured into the bowl.

> "Holy God, we ask you to bless us as
> we gather. And we ask you to bless this
> water of life. For it is water that wakes
> the seedling and invites it to grow. It is
> water that reaches even the deepest
> roots to nourish and sustain. It is water
> that refreshes a parched throat. The
> soft sound of a running spring can
> refresh our spirits. We are born in a
> rush of water and reborn in the waters
> of Baptism. We thank you for this great
> gift of water and for your blessing."

Invite all participants to come up to the water and bless themselves.

'The World According to God'

Ask family members to find their own work space. Give each family some markers and a piece of newsprint with a large circle drawn on it. Tell them we are going to spend some time together talking about the Reign of God—what the world would be like if everyone on this earth were living according to God's plan. Ask them to pretend that the large circle on the newsprint is the earth. Ask them to write words or draw symbols inside the circle to show what the world would be like if everyone were living according to God's plan. Give them about fifteen minutes to complete their work.

Sharing Our Worlds

Ask families to gather in the large group. Tell them that you will be talking about sacraments, but first you would like them to share what they have put on the newsprint. Have them hang their "worlds" on the wall. After all of the families have had a chance to present their interpretations of the "world according to God," congratulate them on their good work. Then hang another piece of newsprint with a large circle on it on the wall, close enough to one of the other pieces of newsprint so that later you can tape a poster board bridge to connect the two.

Ask families to help you fill out this world with word or symbols that show what the world is really like today. Make sure that, along with the good things that are said about our world, you also include such issues as poverty, hunger, violence, greed, prejudice and pollution. Ask participants what they think the real world needs to help it become more like the world they envisioned on newsprint.

You hope that, in one way or another, they will say that the world needs people to start working together to stop evil and help bring about good. In your own words tell them the following:

"This was what Jesus was about. Wherever he went, evil was destroyed and good things happened. Jesus' mission was to proclaim the Good News—to set things right, to reconcile the world, so that the world could begin to live according to God's plan. The Reign of God began when Jesus, the Son of God, entered into the world and become a part of its history.

"What an extraordinary event! For a very little while, God was with us in a very special, visible, concrete way. Jesus fed the hungry, stopped violence, healed, forgave and empowered the suffering. For three years, wherever Jesus went, he lived out the plan of God.

"There were, however, people who hated Jesus. They arrested him, beat him and had him killed. But even death had no power over him. In three days, Jesus rose from the dead. And the world will never be the same again.

"At Pentecost, the Spirit of God descended on Jesus' disciples. God's power was unleashed and the Church was born. Once more the Body of Christ was present to the world in a visible, concrete way. The Church was commissioned to carry on Jesus' mission of proclaiming the Good News, to reconcile the world in peace and harmony, to destroy evil and make good things happen. This is the Church we are baptized into. And through our Baptism we become a part of the Body of Christ.

"For centuries the Church has been trying to continue Jesus' mission by taking care of and empowering the broken people of the world, by working against violence and injustice. This, of course, is the Church at its best. Does it always act according to the plan of God? No. The Church is made up of human beings who make mistakes and sin. And so the people of the Church have also been involved in violence (the Crusades, the Inquisition) and injustice (condemning Galileo, allowing slavery). It is up to every generation to make the people of God more like the Body of Christ, the Church it is meant to be. Now it is our turn to carry on Jesus' mission and help bring about the Plan of God."

A Sacrament for the Real World

Take the half piece of poster board and tape it on the wall so that it connects the real world to a newsprint "world according to God's plan." Ask them to help you think of things to write on this bridge, some ways they can help make today's world more the way God wants it to be. Try to help them focus on things they are able to do or ask, "How can you help accomplish this?"

Then say in your own words:

"Imagine an individual trying to do all of these things alone. It would become exhausting and frustrating. One person working alone would burn out in a very short period of time. That is why there is Church. Jesus said he will be 'where two or more are gathered' [see Matthew 18:20]. When we work together we have extra energy and stamina. When we work as Church we have additional strength and power as the Body of Christ. This is what the sacraments do for us: They give us power and strength. When we receive a sacrament, God's very life within us empowers us. And this is how these things [point to poster board bridge] can happen.

"Let's take a couple of steps back now and look at what a sacrament is. One way of explaining a sacrament is to say that *a sacrament is a visible, concrete, effective sign of God's presence with us and in us*. If we understand sacraments in this way, we can see that Jesus was the perfect sacrament. He was the living, breathing presence of God with us, among us, an intimate part of who we are. And the Church, the Body of Christ, is the primary sacrament—a living, visible sign of God's continued presence in the world.

"Finally, there are the sacraments that we receive individually, seven special gifts dispensed by the Church. They are visible, concrete signs that God's life is in us. They are peak moments when the Church recognizes and celebrates with us our own intimate relationship with God. The sacraments—Baptism, Confirmation, Eucharist, Penance, Anointing of the Sick, Holy Orders and Matrimony— mark the important stages in the life of a Christian They are gifts, power coming forth (see *CCC* #1116) to initiate, strengthen, nurture, comfort and empower us, as we continue within the Body of Christ to live out Jesus' mission to proclaim in word and action the Good News, destroying evil and making good things happen."

Break

Take ten minutes to get refreshments, use the restrooms or just walk around a bit and mingle.

Oil Ritual

Ask participants to gather once more around the table that holds the bowl of water blessed in the previous ritual and the candle. Next to the bowl place a cruet or a small clear cream pitcher with oil in it and the small paper cups you cut down—one for each family. Raise your right hand over the oil, asking others to do the same, and pray this blessing:

"Holy God, we ask you to bless this oil so that it may heal and strengthen us and remind us we are part of your royal family, a priestly people."

Ask someone who is a good reader to read 1 Samuel 16:3-13. (Give them time to look it over beforehand.) Begin by saying,

"We are going to begin with a reading from the First Book of Samuel."

After Scripture is read, slowly pour the oil from the cruet into each of the small cups. When the reading is finished, say in your own words:

"Samuel anointed David with his family all around him. And from that day on the Spirit of God rushed upon David. Take this oil and bless each other: Children anoint their parents; parents anoint their children."

Show them how to do it by asking someone to come forward. Take a little oil on your thumb and make a small Sign of the Cross on his or her forehead while you say,

"May you be blessed in the name of the Father, and of the Son, and of the Holy Spirit."

Ask the parents to come forward and receive a cup of oil for their family. You might want to play some quiet music while they are blessing each other. When they are finished, ask them to pour any remaining oil back into the cruet.

Water

Genesis 2:10
John 3:5
Proverbs 25:25
Leviticus 16:24
Exodus 14:26-29

Oil

Ezekiel 16:13
Psalm 104:15
Luke 10:34
Exodus 27:20
1 Samuel 10:1

Bread

Jeremiah 37:21
Leviticus 24:5-9
1 Corinthians 10:17
Luke 14:15
Luke 4:3

The Sacraments of Initiation

Begin by saying in your own words:

"Today we are going to look at the first three sacraments, the sacraments of initiation: Baptism, Confirmation and Eucharist. And we are going to begin by looking at the visible, concrete signs that symbolize them: water, oil and bread."

Divide those gathered into groups of five to six people of varied ages. Give each group one of the lists of Scripture references below. Tell them they are to look up the passages to discover the various uses and varieties of the symbol they will be working on. When they are finished looking up the readings, they are to make a collage with pictures and words cut from magazines that depicts and celebrates their symbol. They may also draw or write things on their poster board. Show them where all the supplies are. Give them thirty minutes to work together. Go up to the group that is working with the symbol of bread and let them know you realize there are not that many different uses; they may want to make a collage that focuses on the great variety of breads.

Signs and Symbols

Begin with the symbol of water. Ask the groups who worked with this symbol to tell the rest of the participants the various uses of water. Give them some time to walk around and show the collage they have put together. Follow the same process with the other symbols, oil and bread. If you still have some wall space left, hang up the collages.

Distribute the Handout Page "Signs and Symbols." Say something like the following:

"One of the important thing to remember about sacraments is that they are not 'just signs'; they are symbols. Like signs, they are always visible and concrete. Unlike signs, they not only announce what is happening (God lives within us), they also bring it about. Look over the handout you just received and see if you can tell me what the drawings mean.

"Stop sign, no-smoking sign and exit sign are obvious. They are visible things you can touch that tell you what actions may or may not be taken, but they do not make those things happen. The parent hugging a child and a child giving an adult some flowers are more obscure. They are actions (visible and concrete) that can convey many meanings: 'I love you' or 'I am sorry.' The hug and the flowers are not only signs of love or a need for forgiveness, they are also ways of making it happen.

"Now let us talk about the signs and symbols you just finished working with. We will begin with water."

Write the following on newsprint:

Through Baptism
1) We are initiated into the Church and become members of the Body of Christ.
2) All our past sins are washed away.
3) The old self dies and we become a new person in Christ.

Ask, "How can water symbolize these experiences of Baptism?" Some possible answers are:

1) We come into this world as infants who have been immersed in water. It is fitting that water is also a symbol of our new birth as members of the Body of Christ.
2) Water is used for cleansing and is a good symbol for washing away our sins.
3) Just as all Pharaoh's army died in the Red Sea, our immersion in water symbolizes the dying of our old selves. When we come up from the water we live again in Christ.

Continue with the symbol of oil, a symbol for both Baptism and Confirmation. Put up newsprint with the following:

In Baptism and Confirmation
1) We are strengthened by the gift of the fullness of the Holy Spirit.
2) We become a priestly people.
3) Our understanding is enlightened.

Ask, "How can oil symbolize these effects of Baptism and Confirmation?" Some possible answers are:

1) Oil was used by athletes to help strengthen them.
2) Priests and holy people in biblical times were often anointed.
3) Oil is used in lamps for light.

Finally, look at the Sacrament of the Eucharist. Put up the newsprint with the following on it:

In the Eucharist
1) It is our most important spiritual nourishment, the Body and Blood of Christ.
2) It celebrates our oneness with Christ and each other.
3) It is an action of thanksgiving.

Ask those gathered, "How can bread symbolize these effects of Eucharist?" Some possible answers are:

1) Bread is an important source of nourishment in many parts of the world.
2) Baked bread is made up of many grains of wheat, oil and water that become one loaf. Even when bread is broken, it still remains the bread from one loaf.
3) Bread itself symbolizes all of our daily needs. When we ask for our daily bread in the Our Father we are asking for all the necessities of the day.

Bread Ritual

Ask everyone to gather in the prayer space again. This time place beside the candle, water and oil a loaf of bread on a plate or in a small low basket. Say the following in your own words:

"At Eucharist, ordinary bread is broken and shared. Consecrated, it becomes the Body and Blood of Christ. Today we will take this ordinary bread. We will bless it and break it. It will remain bread, but our blessing will make it sacred. Each of you will get a piece of the bread big enough to share with those around you. When everyone has received their piece stand up and share your bread. This is what you will do."

Model the procedure with a volunteer as you explain,

"Go up to someone and break off a piece of their bread and eat it, as he or she breaks off and eats a piece of yours. Exchange a greeting of peace, a 'thank you' or some other appropriate comment. Then go on to another individual, doing the same until all your bread is gone. At that time return to your seat."

Make sure everyone understands before you begin. When there are no more questions pray the following blessing:

"We ask you, great God, to bless this bread. Make it a sign of our oneness. Help it to nourish our spirits as it nourishes our bodies. Help us to see you in the faces of those with whom we break bread. Bless us as we share this symbol of your great abundance."

Break the bread into enough pieces so that everyone has a piece. You might want to play soft music while they share the broken bread. When everyone is finished say the following,

"One of our very first prayers as a people of faith was the Our Father. Now let us say together this most precious prayer of our Church."

Signs and Symbols

Further Resources From St. Anthony Messenger Press

Catholic Update and *Scripture From Scratch* are four-page, popularly written publications from St. Anthony Messenger Press/Franciscan Communications. Although some basic theology is presented on each Grown-up's Page, consider sending some of these titles home for the adults participating in the program.

The letter *C* at the beginning of the order number identifies *Catholic Update*; the letter *N*, *Scripture From Scratch*. Both can be ordered from St. Anthony Messenger Press/Franciscan Communications, 1615 Republic Street, Cincinnati, OH 45210. Call toll-free 1-800-488-0488; FAX 1-513-241-1197.

Yahweh Calls

"The Bible From Square One" (N0794)
"Finding Your Way Through the Old Testament" (C1189)
"The Creation Story of Genesis" (C0694)
"Abraham" (N1096)
"Moses: The Man Who Knew the Lord Face to Face" (N1096)
"The Ten Commandments: Sounds of Love From Sinai" (C0989)
"Exodus and Exile: Shaping God's People" (N0295)
"David: Israel's Poet King" (N0595)
"Biblical Prophets: Challenging Role Models" (N0994)
"Kaleidoscope of Biblical Women" (N0395)

Jesus Lives

"The Four Faces of Jesus" (C0390)
"Who Is Jesus?" (C0985)
"Christmas Story: Exploring the Gospel Infancy Narratives" (N1294)
"It's a Miracle! Signs and Wonders in Scripture" (N0995)
"Tantalizing Parables Jesus Told" (N1293)
"The Creed: Faith Essentials for Catholics" (C0785)
"Our Father: The Prayer Jesus Taught Us" (C1296)
"The Beatitudes: Finding Where Your Treasure Is" (C1291)
"The Passion Narratives: The Cross Takes Center Stage" (N0294)
"Resurrection Stories: Catching the Light of God's Love" (N0394)

Spirit With Us

"Who Is the Holy Spirit?" (C0695)
"The Holy Spirit: Yesterday and Today" (C0595)
"Sacraments: It All Starts With Jesus" (C0893)
"The Seven Sacraments: Symbols of God's Care" (C0483)
"Sacrament of Baptism: Celebrating the Embrace of God" (C0389)
"Real Presence in the Eucharist" (C0996)
"A Walk Through the Mass" (C0889)
"Sacrament of Reconciliation: Celebrating God's Forgiveness" (C0386)
"Works of Mercy: Jesus' Plan for Social Change" (C1093)
"What Is the Kingdom of God?" (C0980)